ASYLUM

WILLIAM SEABROOK

INTRODUCTION AND NEW COVER BY
JOE OLLMANN

DOVER PUBLICATIONS, INC.
MINEOLA, NEW YORK

Bibliographical Note

This Dover edition, first published in 2015, is an unabridged republication of the work originally published by Harcourt, Brace and Company, New York, in 1935. A new introduction by Joe Ollmann has been specially prepared for this edition.

Library of Congress Cataloging-in-Publication Data

Seabrook, William, 1884–1945.
 Asylum / William Seabrook ; introduction and new cover by Joe Ollmann.
  pages cm
 "Unabridged republication of the work originally published by Harcourt, Brace and Company, New York, in 1935"—Title page verso.
 ISBN-13: 978-0-486-79810-3 (paperback)
 ISBN-10: 0-486-79810-0 (paperback)
 1. Seabrook, William, 1884–1945—Health. 2. Alcoholism—Hospitals—New York (State)—Westchester County—History—20th century. 3. Alcoholics—Rehabilitation—New York (State)—Westchester County—History—20th century. 4. Mentally ill—Care—New York (State)—Westchester County—History—20th century. 5. Alcoholics—New York (State)—Westchester County—Biography. 6. Psychotherapy patients—New York (State)—Westchester County—Biography. I. Title.
RC564.74.N7S43 2015
362.29209747'277—dc23

2015006988

Manufactured in the United States
79810003   2016
www.doverpublications.com

YOU ALL KNOW WILLIAM SEABROOK, RIGHT?

WILLIAM SEABROOK... HE BROUGHT THE WORD *ZOMBIE* INTO THE ENGLISH LANGUAGE.

the MAGIC ISLAND BY WILLIAM SEABROOK

HIS BOOK, *THE MAGIC ISLAND*, WAS THE BASIS OF *WHITE ZOMBIE*, STARRING BELA LUGOSI, THE FIRST-EVER ZOMBIE MOVIE!

WHITE ZOMBIE

IT COULD BE ARGUED THAT SEABROOK IS RESPONSIBLE FOR THE WHOLE ZOMBIE PHENOMENA. **THAT** WILLIAM SEABROOK. NO?

ZOMBIE

NIGHT OF THE LIVING DEAD

EVIL DEAD THE ORIGINAL

ZOMBIE, THE COCKTAIL

MAYBE YOU'RE MORE HIGHBROW. THIS IS THE GUY WHO WAS CLOSE FRIENDS WITH SINCLAIR LEWIS, ALDOUS HUXLEY AND THOMAS MANN.

HE KNEW DASHIELL HAMMETT AND GERTRUDE STEIN TOO... HE SMOKED OPIUM WITH JEAN COCTEAU, COLLABORATED ON A PHOTO SERIES WITH MAN RAY AND WAS WORKING ON A BALLET WITH SALVADOR DALI.

SEABROOK!

SURELY YOU'VE HEARD OF THIS GUY? WILLIAM SEABROOK, THE EXPLORER... LIVED WITH BEDOUIN TRIBESMEN, AND A HAITIAN WITCH DOCTOR, AND WITH GUERRE CANNIBALS!

HELL, HE **WAS** A CANNIBAL THAT ONE TIME...

HMM... TASTES LIKE VEAL.

("NECK-MEAT" FROM A MORGUE!)

HE PRACTICED BLACK MAGIC WITH ALEISTER CROWLEY AND HE WAS ALSO A BONDAGE ENTHUSIAST.

(FROM A MAN RAY PHOTO OF SEABROOK AND LEE MILLER)

HE WAS ALSO ONE OF THE BEST-KNOWN, HIGHEST-PAID WRITERS OF HIS TIME. YOU KNOW: WILLIAM SEABROOK!

SIGH...

YEAH... WILLIAM SEABROOK IS VIRTUALLY UNKNOWN TODAY. NONE OF HIS ELEVEN BOOKS REMAINED IN PRINT. UNTIL NOW... WITH THIS NEW DOVER EDITION OF ASYLUM. YAY!

TOO OFTEN, SEABROOK IS REDUCED TO THIS FOUR-WORD BIOGRAPHY: CANNIBAL, SADIST, ALCOHOLIC, SUICIDE...

CANNIBAL SADIST ALCOHOLIC SUICIDE

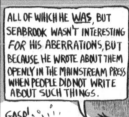

ALL OF WHICH HE WAS, BUT SEABROOK WASN'T INTERESTING FOR HIS ABERRATIONS, BUT BECAUSE HE WROTE ABOUT THEM OPENLY IN THE MAINSTREAM PRESS WHEN PEOPLE DID NOT WRITE ABOUT SUCH THINGS.

GASP!

IT MAY HAVE BEEN HIS DOWN-FALL IN THE END, THIS CANDOR.

HMMPH!

ASYLUM WAS WRITTEN WHEN SEABROOK—WITH THE HELP OF HIS PUBLISHER, ALFRED KNOPF, WAS COMMITTED TO BLOOM-INGDALE MENTAL HOSPITAL TO CURE HIS ALCOHOLISM.

BLOOMINGDALE INSANE ASYLUM
↑
(ACTUAL FACILITY NAME)

AT THAT TIME, 1939, SEABROOK WAS LIVING IN TOULON, FRANCE, IN A CONVERTED ONION WARE-HOUSE WHICH BELONGED TO FORD MADOX FORD'S WIFE.

HIS FIRST THREE TRAVEL/ADVEN-TURE BOOKS HAD BEEN BEST-SELLERS, HAD BEEN LUCRA-TIVELY SERIALIZED IN MAIN-STREAM MAGAZINES AND SEABROOK WAS SUFFERING ALL OF THE EXCESSES OF SUCCESS.

HE WAS AT A DANGEROUS STAGE OF ALCOHOLISM AND WAS COMPLETELY BLOCKED IN WRITING *THE WHITE MONK OF TIMBUCTOO*, AN UNINSPIRED SPIN-OFF PROJECT FROM HIS EARLIER TRIPS TO AFRICA.

HE WAS DRINKING EVERYTHING AND WRITING NOTHING, AND IT WAS KILLING HIM.

"SO LONG AS A MAN DRINKS WHEN HE WANTS AND STOPS WHEN HE WANTS TO, HE ISN'T A DRUNKARD."

BUT HE HAD LONG AGO PASSED THE POINT OF STOPPING WHEN HE WANTED.

HE TOOK WHAT WAS THEN THE RADICAL STEP OF SEEKING A CURE FOR ALCOHOLISM IN A MENTAL HEALTH FACILITY AT A TIME WHEN HABITUAL DRUNKARDS WERE TREATED FOR THEIR PHYSICAL SYMPTOMS ONLY...

...WHILE THEIR PSYCHOLOGICAL CONDITIONS, THE *REASONS* THEY DRANK, WERE NEVER TOUCHED UPON.

THE TWO BOOKS HE PRODUCED PRIOR TO *ASYLUM* SUFFERED FOR NOT BEING FIRST-PERSON DOCUMENTS OF EXPEDITIONS INTO UNKNOWN TERRITORIES AS HIS EARLIER BESTSELLERS HAD BEEN.

A PAMPERED TRAVELOGUE OF A WEALTHY WRITER FLYING TO AFRICA

PROFILE OF A DRUNKEN, DEFROCKED MONK IN AFRICA.

AIR ADVENTURE
SEABROOK

THE WHITE MONK OF TIMBUCTOO
SEABROOK

FROM THE BEGINNING, SEABROOK TREATED HIS COMMITTAL TO A MENTAL HOSPITAL AS AN EXPEDITION TO A NEW FRONTIER AND ITS INHABITANTS WERE "THE NATIVES."

HIS SECOND WIFE, THE WRITER MARJORIE WORTHINGTON, DESCRIBED PACKING THE SAME SUPPLIES FOR BLOOMINGDALES THAT HE TOOK WITH HIM ON SAFARI.

ALL OF WHICH MADE *ASYLUM* A RETURN TO FORM, AND AS AN ETHNOGRAPHIC STUDY, IT STANDS WITH THE BEST OF HIS TRAVEL BOOKS.

HE CAREFULLY DOCUMENTED HIS WITHDRAWAL AND PHYSICAL CURE AND HIS ATTEMPTS TO FIND THE ROOT CAUSES OF HIS DRINKING PROBLEM.

I MUST WRITE ABOUT THIS LATER...

AT THE END OF THE BOOK, A SOBER SEABROOK WAXES PHILOSOPHICALLY IF HE COULD TAKE A DRINK OR NOT NOW THAT HE WAS "CURED."

LIKE ME, YOU MAY FIND YOURSELF FEELING LIKE YOU ARE WATCHING A HORROR MOVIE AT THIS POINT, "DON'T OPEN THAT DOOR, WILLIE!" KNOWING HOW TEMPORARY HIS CURE WAS TO BE IN THE END.

NO!

ASYLUM HAS ALL OF THE FRANK HONESTY, OPENNESS AND FERVENT INTEREST IN PEOPLE, COUPLED WITH A LACK OF JUDGEMENT, THAT WAS A FEATURE OF THE BEST OF SEABROOK'S WRITING.

IT'S ALSO A DETAILED PORTRAIT OF DAILY LIFE INSIDE A "MENTAL HOSPITAL," THE ECCENTRICITIES OF BOTH PATIENTS AND STAFF, ARCHAIC PSYCHOLOGY TERMS LIKE NEURASTHENIA AND DEMENTIA PRAECOX, AND SEVERAL ACTUAL CLICHÉD NAPOLEON COMPLEXES...

CLASHES BETWEEN INFLEXIBLE STAFF AND A STUBBORN ICONOCLAST LIKE SEABROOK WERE INEVITABLE AND ARE REMINISCENT OF KESEY'S *ONE FLEW OVER THE CUCKOO'S NEST*.

WITH A DR. QUIGLEY SERVING AS VILLAIN IN PLACE OF NURSE RATCHED.

NO PRUNES FOR YOU, MR. SEABROOK...

SEABROOK FELT THAT HE DRANK BECAUSE OF AN INFERIORITY COMPLEX; THAT HE WAS MERELY A HACK WRITER OF PULPY TRASH WHO STRUGGLED FUTILELY TO BE MORE.

SIGH...

I HOPE THAT AT THE END OF HIS LIFE HE MIGHT HAVE LOOKED BACK AT *ASYLUM* FONDLY.

"IF SOME LIVING PEOPLE CONTINUE TO READ YOUR WORDS, YOU REMAIN ALIVE."

NOW IT'S TIME TO ENTER *ASYLUM*...

iv

AUTHOR'S NOTE

None of this book is fiction or embroidery. It is not a novel. It is straight fact. All the characters and episodes are real, but all proper names, except my own, whether of fellow-patients, places, doctors or attendants, have been completely changed.

PREFACE

"Acute alcoholism" was the way my commitment read, to which was added when the doctors and psychiatrists had checked me over:

"Chronic

"Neurasthenic symptoms; marked

"Psychopathic symptoms; zero."

This was in the winter of 1933 when friends succeeded, just before Christmas, in having me committed, through the New York courts, for treatment and possible cure, to one of the oldest and largest insane asylums in the East.[1]

I had asked for it. I mean, I had asked for it literally, though I hadn't specified any particular sort of place. I had been begging, pleading, demanding toward the last, to be locked up . . . shut up . . . chained up . . . anything . . . and had begun to

[1] They now call it a "mental hospital," as all such places do—but asylum is still what everybody knows it is, and it proved so truly an "asylum" for me that I have a friendly feeling for the good old word. Asylum from the storm; sanctuary; refuge. That's what the dictionary says the word still means, primarily. That's what it meant to me. That's why I don't mind using it. That's why I call this book *Asylum.*

curse and blame my dearest friends for what seemed to me their failure to realize how desperately, how stupidly, I needed to be shut up where I couldn't get out and where I couldn't get my hands on a bottle.

I had become a confirmed, habitual drunkard, without any of the stock alibis, or excuses. My health was otherwise excellent; I had plenty of money in the bank, a pleasant home on the French Riviera; my work had been going well enough until the drink put an end to it and promised soon to put an end to me. Then I had tried to stop—and couldn't. I knew that I was killing myself by drinking, and I did not want to die.

I was pragmatic about it, with a lucid, drunken, persistent, one-track clarity. I had "direction." My direction brought me back to the United States, to my own country, obsessed with the specific desire to be put behind bars where I couldn't get liquor, and where, if I changed my mind, I couldn't wheedle or bribe my jailors, or break the bars down. I never once blamed cognac, wine, or whiskey. I blamed myself, with anger—and disgust. I wanted to be cured, if cure were possible . . . but I perhaps also wanted to be punished. There was perhaps a twisted puritanical, or perhaps even definitely masochistic, quirk in my wish to

be locked up, but I think there was an intuitive element of survival-wish in it too. I knew, better than
any of my friends did—for they seldom saw me
maudlin and never saw me violent—that I had already
slipped past the point where any sanitarium, hospital,
treatment or environment which depended on my voli-
tional coöperation, could hold out any hope. I knew
that I had lost my will with relation to alcohol. I
knew that there was only left to me the wish—which
is entirely different from the will—to be saved from
my own weakness. I repeat here, just as I repeated to
my friends, over and over again until they and I were
sick of it, that I knew I was drinking myself to death,
that I couldn't stop—and that I wanted to be stopped
—by force.

It seems, however, that this had presented to my
friends a somewhat more difficult problem than I realized, particularly since I had no immediate surviving
family—father, mother, brother, blood relations—with
direct legal authority to do anything about it. There
is no law anyway—and of course there shouldn't be
any—to stop a man from drinking himself to death if
he doesn't disturb the public peace. And it seems that
it is against the criminal law for private individuals,

even family or doctors, to lock up or chain up an individual without due legal process—even though the individual invites it.

Fortunately I found one friend who was capable enough, influential enough and hard-boiled enough to "call" what might have been a hysterical bluff and hand me the big-league works tied up with a piece of strong red tape and signed by a judge who had never heard of me.

I was a little surprised.

The friend said:

"You know, this isn't Arabia or the moon, or the Sixteenth Century, or a novel by the Marquis de Sade. It's the free United States of America in 1933. The big psychopathic institutions are not very keen on taking drunks, but times are hard and their entrance requirements are not quite so strict as they used to be. If you are willing to sign this court commitment yourself, I can get you into —— tomorrow."

My friend named a place so big and so universally known that its proper name was once a vaudeville synonym for the sort of place it is. I was a little surprised, not having thought precisely of that sort of place, and it also surprised some devoted but less hard-boiled friends who were present, with my welfare at heart. I gulped down the rest of a big drink of prescription Scotch—it was in a penthouse overlooking Gramercy Park on the night before the repeal of the dry law—and said:

"Okay. Send for the wagon and net."

I was locked up in ——— next day, and kept locked up there for seven months. It proved a queer way to be locked up, for pretty soon I walked miles in the snow whether I wanted to or not, went regularly to the barber shop whether I wanted to or not, went to dances and movies whether I wanted to or not, was made to play golf and tennis when spring came, was taken on hikes in woods full of pheasants, quail, and rabbits—yet all this time I was locked up—and competently. It put no strain whatever on my drunkard's honor or my drunkard's will. It would have been just about as hard to escape from this place as to escape from Sing Sing, and if I had escaped, I understood that the state police would bring me back—in handcuffs if necessary.

As a matter of fact, for that very reason, I never thought seriously of trying to escape. I puzzled over escaping occasionally, as you puzzle over schemes to steal the British crown jewels after the first time you've seen them in the Tower of London, but it was purely academic, like anagrams or crossword puzzles. I felt occasionally, less academically, that I'd like to wreck the dump, but that was before I began to understand what it was all about. It wouldn't have made any difference. They were prepared for that!

In July they let me out, with handshakes and good-natured kidding, through the main gate. From first to last it was the most fantastic and not-at-all-as-I-had-expected experience in my life up to now. Its tempo, atmosphere, and daily rituals—particularly since I had all the usual, preconceived wrong notions of what goes on in such a place—were even stranger than the novitiate I once undertook in a Whirling Dervish monastery.

Incidentally they seem to have cured me, which is as may be. I hope they have, and I hope too that an honest account of my experience may be of some use. I am sure there must be innumerable families who feel like doing something fairly desperate to save Uncle John or Brother Charlie from the well-known "drunkard's grave," but who would actually rather "see him in his grave" than shut up in a "madhouse." I believe this medieval attitude is nonsense today, and one idea I have in writing this adventure is to show what nonsense it is. But since I intend to be honest, I may as well admit that such motives are incidental. I am not a reformer of public opinion, or a propagandist. I am an adventure writer of sorts, and I write this mainly as the story of a strange adventure in a strange place.

W. B. S.

Rhinebeck, N. Y.
January, 1935.

ASYLUM

I

ONE THING they don't punish you for is swearing at the doctors. I didn't know this. So when I did it I wasn't abusing a privilege. I didn't know anything yet—except that everything was all wrong. One of the big ones with a belly and a beard, oozing authority, had come around after breakfast, and I was telling him.

"For Christ's sake," I said, "what kind of a dump is this? I came here for seclusion. I came here to be locked up. I thought I had rented a nice, quiet cell. And you stick me in a wide-open show window, in a God-damned illuminated dog kennel without any front where people come walking in and out and prodding me with sticks every minute of the day and night. I spent a hell of a night. And just now, by God, they chased me out of that hole and made me come out here in this public movie lobby while they change the straw, or make the bed, or something."

I had been brought in late the previous afternoon,

polite, quiet, articulate, and able to walk without stag-
gering, but drunk as a Bandusian goat, and now, after
some black coffee which hadn't stayed down and a
cigarette which tasted awful, I should have been pour-
ing myself a half tumbler of Scotch if I had been back
in the penthouse, but I was so astonished at what had
been happening to me, so resentful and angry, that I
wasn't even thinking about liquor—for the moment.
I was thinking that my friends had muffed it again,
and of telephoning them to come and get me out. I
was thinking, and getting sorer every minute, of what
had happened since they had left me.

They had left me in the outer office—or rather I
had left them—after we had sat around nervously,
talked to some doctors, smoked cigarettes, and signed
some more papers. A pretty little red-haired woman,
plump, trim, smooth, and sandy, like a nice apple
dumpling, a sort of musical comedy, pocket-edition,
prison matron with a bunch of keys chained to her belt,
came and stood like bait in the doorway.

I said my friends would just come along and see me
settled.

No? We would say good-by here?

Well, my one friend would just come along and see
that everything was all right.

No, everything was already settled. Everything was all right. I would just tell them good-by and go along now with Miss Baxter.

But my handbag, my pajamas, a detective story that . . . ?

No, all that would be attended to. No, I needn't bother about my hat and overcoat. I would just go along now with Miss Baxter.

I felt in my pocket to be sure I had cigarettes and my lighter, said good-by to my friends, and went with Miss Baxter. She didn't say anything. She led me through a long hall like a hotel lobby, richly carpeted in red, with pictures and steel engravings of the Parthenon, King Lear's daughters and William Tell. We walked the length of a city block and turned a corner and kept walking along a continuation of the same hall for another block or so until she came to a heavy door, and we were now in another corridor, narrower and barer, which went on in the same endless way.

She walked briskly ahead, sometimes glancing back or dropping back beside me. She was pretty and I thought I'd like to say something to her. There were red lights over some of the doors and I thought of saying something that I decided not to say. I said instead:

"I see you've got traffic signals. Why didn't we take a taxi?"

She smiled mechanically and said, "Yes."

After passing through more doors and finally unlocking a heavy double one, and walking what seemed a mile or so more, we came to another long hall, a corridor wing, furnished like a Radio City lounge or Peacock Alley in the old Waldorf, including the grand piano, except that it had a lot of open bedrooms opening off it on both sides; a small blond young man in white said, "My name's Gilmore; how do you do, Mr. Seabrook," and a big dark young prize-fighter in ordinary clothes but with a white jacket said, "My name's Dan; how do you do, Mr. Seabrook," while Miss Baxter melted away.

I had never walked so far under one roof since I'd visited the Palace of Versailles. I said to them, since I supposed I was supposed to say something:

"Break out of here? Why, a guy couldn't *find* his way out unless he hired a Cook's guide."

They both smiled mechanically and said, "Yes."

I learned weeks later that they'd both written it down that same night in my chart-book. They write down anything a patient says about death, escape, or suicide, whether it seems to make sense or not. The first thing written about me was that I was thinking of escaping by bribing the attendants.

I had been drinking since seven that morning, even more conscientiously than usual, knowing it would be the last for a long while. My friends had not interfered. What difference did one last day make? I had finished a pint before they came to get me, and had finished the last of a second pint in the car coming out. I had been so continually soaked with it for nearly two years that it didn't make me shout or sing or want to fight. It was about six o'clock now, of a winter evening, December, 1933, a couple of hours since I'd had the last drink, and I was beginning to sink. When they showed me to one of the open bedrooms, I flopped down on the bed. They were saying something, politely, when I went to sleep or passed out.

I guess they wakened me in a little while. The blond one who said his name was something had a pair of my pajamas, slippers, and dressing gown. The big one who said his name was something else helped me undress. I went to sleep or passed out again.

In what might have been a minute or an hour, the big one alone was shaking me, and telling me that I would have a nice shower now and get weighed. I had been so habitually, normally drunk all the time for so long a time, that when I wasn't completely unconscious I focused better than occasional drunks do. I told him that I never took showers at night and that I weighed a hundred and eighty-nine pounds. He looked at me, sizing me up, then suddenly turned human and stopped calling me Mr. Seabrook and said, "Come on, fellow, I'll help you; I can't help it, you know, it's the rules."

And when I wouldn't, he went away, but before I could go to sleep or pass out again, he was back with another older man in a white uniform who didn't look exactly like a nurse or like a doctor either, who said:

"My-name-is-Dirk-how-do-you-do-Mr.-Seabrook; sorry, but it's the rules that all patients who *walk* in must have a bath and be weighed the same day they come in."

I said, "Who in the hell are you?" and he said, "I'm the superintendent on this hall. Come on. We'll help you. But you don't want us to *take* you."

I had never been a fighting drunk, so I went along. I thought they would let me alone for the rest of the night.

The next one who waked me up was a young female nurse with a tray who said:

"I'm-Miss-Pine-how-do-you-do-Mr.-Seabrook; how would you like some supper?"

I said:

"For the love of God take it away, and stop calling me by my name like a Statler hotel parrot, and since you look like you might have a kind heart, please shut the door when you go out and tell that army out there to let me alone until morning."

She said she was sorry, it was against the rules to shut the door, but if I didn't want my supper wouldn't I sleep better if I had a glass of milk and some crackers?

When she went out, I got up and shut the door myself and noticed that it had no lock on it and turned off the overhead light which worked by a button near the door and went to bed and noticed that the room was still suffused with a blue light. It was coming from a hole in the wall protected by heavy glass and grating so that you couldn't break it or turn it off. I pushed a chair against it, with my bathrobe draped so that it made the room dark.

In a little while a new male one, who didn't say his name was anything or how do you do, tiptoed in, removed the chair and bathrobe and left the door wide open.

I said loudly, "For the love of Christ can't you even let a guy . . ."

He said, "Rules. Not so loud please, you'll wake the other patients."

I said, "Do you mean to tell me anybody *sleeps* in this God-damned bughouse?"

He went out and I lay for what might have been an hour or so and went to sleep again and woke up again, and the bright electric light was on and another new male one was there with a bottle of vaseline and some thermometers and a watch.

He told me I'd be let alone from then on, and presently, though I noticed there was another one reading a book, with a shaded lamp, in the corridor across from my door, I passed out again and was asleep or unconscious for what seemed forever, until I awoke with a flashlight in my face and standing over me was the biggest one I had seen yet, all in white, but big as one of the Fifth Avenue traffic cops. He was certainly worth looking at, when he moved the light out of my eyes so I could see him. He looked like something out of a good murder drama or the Big House, but now on the side of the law, hard-boiled but melancholy. He should have had a nightstick and a badge and an automatic, but he hadn't, and his pockets weren't bulging. All he had beside his big flashlight was a glass eye. My playmates told me later that a fellow on one of the "back halls" [1] had taken his real eye as a souvenir, and many of the nurses believed this too. Officially he was supposed to have lost it in the Saint Mihiel salient. Neither story was true. His name was Tibbett and he was the night superintendent (which means night watchman) of the whole works. His duty was to look at each patient in the whole rambling "hospital" at least once in the night to make sure they weren't dead or something. I swore at him that first night, but he was all right. He would have been a good person to write a book about. We lent each other lots of books later, all crime stories.

When he continued on his round, after flashing his light in my face, I was more irritated than I'd been when he was there. I began to think that if it had been a mistake to put me in precisely this sort of place, the mistake would soon rectify itself. If I had to spend many nights like this, I'd soon be raving and foaming at the mouth.

---

[1] AUTHOR'S NOTE: Their official designation was "disturbed halls," but the doctors tried in vain to make us drop our slang name for them.

The culmination was when the one with the vaseline and thermometer came back while it was still
pitch-black dark ˋoutside the window and blazed the
light on and said brightly, "Good morning," and I
heard a carpet-sweeper in the hall, and asked him
what time it was and he said, "Six o'clock," and I said,
"What time is breakfast?" and he said, "Quarter to
eight," and when he had pulled the thermometer out
of me and read it I said, "Well, for Christ's sake, get
me a cup of strong black coffee," and he said, "Maybe
you could have a glass of warm milk but you'd have
to see Mr. Dirk and he won't be on till seven."

So that by eight-thirty when the doctor came around
and asked me how I had spent the night, I was so mad
that for the time being I forgot all about being a
drunkard, and was so exhausted and stimulated by
rage that the missing customary morning half-tumbler
of Scotch wasn't even present in the back of my head.
It couldn't have been a deliberate part of their psychic
therapy, but it worked that way. They had eventually
brought my breakfast, and I had drunk some coffee
and eaten part of a piece of toast. I hadn't wanted to
dress, but I noticed that I couldn't have dressed any-
how. All my clothes had disappeared. I had looked in
the wardrobe and bureau drawers. They were all stark

empty. Everything else had disappeared too—my
wrist watch, lighter, matches, cigarette case, pocket-
knife, a medal of Saint Christopher. As for my handbag containing safety-razor, toilet articles, toothbrush,
etc., I never saw it until seven months later. Just now
the only things left in my room were the pajamas I
had slept in, slippers, and bathrobe from which I noticed the tasseled cord had disappeared. Later that
morning I found on the bare, empty bureau my own
toothbrush and paste, in an unbreakable mug, and beside it my spectacles and the half-finished detective
story. Underneath the mug was a penciled note, addressed to nobody and signed by nobody, saying that
they hadn't found any comb or brush. A nurse, who
wouldn't have been there if Mack Sennett had seen
her first, came in and said I would now go out in the
lounge. I said I would stay in my room, but would she
please find my cigarettes, or give me one, and a light.
She said I would now go out in the lounge, but that I
couldn't smoke in my room anyway, and that she
would give me a cigarette and a light when we got out
there. I asked what about my clothes and she said they
had been sent to be marked, but that I didn't need
them now. I said, well, I'd stay in my room until my
clothes came back. She said that I would now go out

in the lounge. She was as hard as Peggy Joyce used to be and nearly as beautiful. She was the same Miss Pine who had brought my supper the night before but I was seeing her for the first time now. I wondered if they were all like that, and if it was part of the treatment.

She talked out of the corner of her mouth, as if she meant it to be tough, but as if she were play-acting it as nurses do when they want to make children obey.

I followed her down the long corridor past other bedrooms to where it spread out, at a right-angle, into a big room which seemed to be a sort of combination smoking room and library, with armchairs, leather couches, long tables with magazines and newspapers, card tables, a big grandfather clock. There were a dozen or so patients who didn't look like patients, fully dressed, flopped here and there, smoking, reading their morning paper, while two white-coated young men hovered unobtrusively, occasionally striking a match to light somebody's cigarette, or do some other trivial services. It was like the lounge of a good hotel—still more like a club. It seemed all very quiet, well-bred, and clubby. Nobody paid any attention to me, except for an occasional glance. Nobody bothered me, or even stared at me, but I resented it nevertheless. For months, since I had been permanently and habitually soused, I had refused to go into places like hotel lobbies where there were people I didn't know. Even aboard the *Europa*, coming back from France, though there happened to be people I knew aboard to whom I could have confessed what ailed me and have been sure of their sympathy, I had stayed in my room with the door shut. I had a neurasthenic—if not actually psychopathic—agoraphobia, the disease opposite of claustrophobia. I wanted to be shut up. I wanted to hide. I wanted to be by myself where people couldn't break in on me. This was, in part, why I had wanted to be locked up, and why the idea of a real big-league modern insane asylum, even though this term was "archaic" and it was now a "mental hospital," had been a welcome idea. Even the idea of a padded cell had been a welcome idea, suggesting seclusion and peace. What I had been subjected to instead for the first twelve hours, is what I have just written here, and what I had been telling the doctor.

He looked at me for a while without saying anything. He looked down at my hands and then looked some more at me, and finally grinned and said:

"Well, that's a new one—if you are not kidding me. We'll try to make you more comfortable, but I am afraid we haven't precisely the accommodation you say you were looking for. The fact is we haven't any cells, padded or otherwise . . ."

"Look here," I said, "I wasn't kidding you, and I don't know whether you are kidding me or not, but, by God, whether you call it a cell or not, you've got to find me a quiet room somewhere, where the door can be shut at night, for I tell you right now that if you think I'm going to stay here another night, commitment or no commitment, if it's going to be like last night was . . ."

"Excuse me," he said, "I must be going along. We'll try to make you as comfortable as we can."

Our conversation had not been in undertones. A patient I was afterward to know as "Spike" slouched over and offered me a cigarette, and said:

"Say, fellow, you've got it all wrong. You don't tell them. They tell you."

II

THE PLACE reminded me increasingly of my mother who believed that by changing the name or appearance of a thing, you could make the thing different—usually better or less worse. A rose by any other name never smelled just as sweet to her. It always smelled sweeter. She was changing sauerkraut into liberty cabbage long before the sinking of the *Lusitania*. A skunk was a wood pussy, and hash became I-don't-remember-what by the addition of a sprig of parsley.

This was not hypocrisy. It was her sincere if sometimes naïve contribution toward making the world happier and brighter. I had affectionately supposed her to be old-fashioned, but I now found the same system at work in this highly scientific, extremely modern institution.

It still seemed to me somewhat naïve, as, for instance, the fiction that we were in a hospital. We all knew the sort of place we were in, and spoke freely about it among ourselves—sometimes humorously and sometimes bitterly—yet always without embarrassment or pretense, but Spike soon cautioned me not to say "college" or "hatch" where any of the doctors or nurses might overhear it. He said it made them feel embarrassed.

And one of the first things I noticed that first morning was that they had tricked up the bars on the windows with my mother's sprig of parsley. They were steel, and a gorilla couldn't have bent them, but they ran in curls and curlycues, like the fancy decorations of a château, looking out on a snow-covered park. If you bit one of the bars, it turned out to be a bar, just as the hash on my mother's table always turned out to be hash when you put your teeth in it, but if you merely sat and looked at it, it looked like something else.

The whole atmosphere of the place was camouflaged in the same kindly way. The nurses, attendants, orderlies in white coats all said, "Yes, Mr. So-and-so," along family hotel lines to make you feel that you were an elegant guest in your own home, and you only discovered that all of them, including the pretty Peggy Joyces, were experts in jiujitsu, if and when you insisted on going to the mat. So that life became a sort of parlor game, like charades or forfeits, and the rules were exactly the same whether you played it with the biggest doctors or the humblest little attendants. The game always began, "My lord, the carriage waits." If that didn't work, they tried polite persuasion, psychology and coaxing. If you insisted, they threw you in. You always went.

For instance, on that very first day I was politely invited to go—and went—to more places than anybody but a Fuller brush salesman ought to visit in a month. I had planned to spend at least a week in bed, or on a cot, tapering off maybe, reading detective stories. I had come here for rest and seclusion. I still had the "nice quiet cell" idea firmly fixed in my mind. Instead, before that first morning ended, they had my tongue hanging out. They had me actually out of breath. The doctors let me alone for the first day, since I had come in voluntarily, under my own steam. But the attendants gave me the works.

It was about nine o'clock in the morning. I was sitting in the movie lobby, smoking another cigarette, waiting to go back to bed. The blond young man who said his name was Gilmore and turned out to be the assistant superintendent of the hall, came and stood politely, pretending to be a solicitous gentleman's gentleman, and informed me deferentially that the barber was ready to shave me. I explained that I always shaved myself, and said, by the way, would he see to it that . . .

He saw to it that . . . I went with him what seemed a mile or two through a lot of corridors and locked doors which he unlocked and locked after us, until he unlocked another and we were in a proper barber shop, with barber's chairs, mirrors, piles of towels, but no rows of bottles or tools in sight, and a barber who said his name was Eddie. Eddie looked at me, saw that I was a new one, unlocked a drawer and selected an old-fashioned razor with a sort of heavy double guard arranged round the blade so that you could give it to a teething baby. I explained that I wasn't anything as interesting as he seemed to think— that I was just a common soak. He said sure, anybody could see that—and proceeded to shave me with the cast iron mouse-trap. They have a holy terror of suicide or attempted suicide, since straitjackets, muffs and handcuffs have been thrown in the discard. It keeps them always on their toes. It was a month before they would even let me have my wrist watch. It seemed absurd, but alcoholics have been known to go off the deep end when they were stopped short, and a piece of broken watch crystal is a nasty gadget.

After I'd been shaved, Gilmore took me for another walk, down through a lot of subterranean passages like the Sewers of Paris, until we came to the baths of Caracalla, very elegant, through lounging rooms with chintz-covered furniture and last year's magazines, a second room with marble cooling boards, and a final room where a fireman stood behind two hoseless nozzles, mounted on a fireboat pedestal with dials and gauges. They stripped me and stood me against the wall where I'd make a fine target, with bars to cling to, so that I wouldn't be knocked down. They gave it to me, first hot, then cold, then hot and cold together. I let out several loud howls, and they laughed. I didn't know whether I was howling because I enjoyed it or because I was outraged. It hit you sometimes like a fist. It was like having a barroom fight with the Johnstown flood. I had come to this place for peace and quiet. I had thought they would give me soothing medicine, mostly in a nice bed, to cure me of the drink habit. And I had signed a court commitment! Now I wanted to escape, but in my drunken state imagined that if I did they'd bring me back escorted by policemen, state troopers, and bloodhounds. I guess I was in a maudlin sort of hangover, for I began to feel sorry enough for myself to burst out crying, and at the same time it was funny.

It soon got funnier. When I was dried and beginning to get my breath back, laid out naked on one of the marble slabs with a pillow under my head, Gilmore and two or three of the other young attendants began to look me over in detail as if I was an exhibit in a dog show. "Good God!" said Gilmore, "look at his toenails! I mean look at the nails on his big toes! Is there a pair of big scissors here?"

I looked too, and it was a fact that they were the longest I'd ever seen on anybody, but they didn't hurt me, and I told them that it was none of their goddamned business how long they were—that this place was supposed to be a bughouse, not a beauty parlor, et cetera.

One of the others said, "Look here, fellow, be reasonable. The doctors'll be stripping you tomorrow, and it won't be you that'll catch hell, it'll be us. Do you want to cut 'em yourself, or shall we cut 'em?"

It hurt my head bending over, and my hands were pretty shaky. Then we resumed Sherman's march through the subterranean tunnels of Torquemada's palace and by the time we reached the next torture-chamber I was out of profanity and breath. I was a mere sick bull with a metaphorical ring in my nose. I shuffled along in my red bedroom slippers. I didn't even have to be pushed. This time, it was a Swedish masseur who had once been a Russian. He knew his business. I must have been in more than a fog than some of my remembering indicates, for I remember that when I asked him what kind of oil he was using he said it was talcum powder, and then I went to sleep while he was still beating me.

When I woke up, they took me into a sort of electric power house where the man who threw the switches patted me on the shoulder so that I wouldn't think of Judd Gray or mistake the X-ray machine for something else, and afterward we went to another office where a woman looked at my teeth as if I were a horse again, and in still another place a young female vampire who later borrowed *Ulysses*, helped herself to as much of my blood as she thought she wanted for the moment, after which we visited the oculist. Eventually young Gilmore decided to call it a morning, and took me back to Hall Four.

It was getting toward noon of the first day. I flopped on my bed and wouldn't get up, and they didn't try to make me. Miss Pine brought me some lunch and let me eat it in bed. I had no appetite and needed a drink pretty desperately, but most of all I was sleepy, exhausted. I don't even remember when she took the tray out. I slept deeply, and if they bothered me I didn't know it. It was getting toward twilight when I awakened sleepily, and soon the big one who looked like a prize-fighter came in with my clothes. He said it was 4:30 and that he would help me dress if I wanted him to. I didn't want him to. I didn't want to dress or be dressed. But what was the use? When I had got dressed, Mr. Dirk, the superintendent, came in to look at me the same way my mother used to look at me on Sunday mornings before church.

And then—it surprised me, yet curiously seemed to be fatal, predestined—he said:

"Don't you think you ought to brush your hair?"

He brought me a comb, and I wet it, sulky and abused, and brushed my hair slick and smooth as an old-fashioned tintype. That seemed to be the way he wanted it, for he rubbed his hands and admired it and said now wouldn't I like to meet the other patients and be shown my seat in the dining room.

I explained—forgetting again the rules of the charade—that I would have my meals in bed for a week or so, and he explained that it would be ever so much nicer to have my meals in the dining room, beginning now.

As a matter of fact, it was not bad, not like a hatch or a hospital either, more like a club restaurant, small tables with flowers. The waiters and waitresses were Mr. Dirk himself, a couple of male nurses, and the beautiful Miss Pine. The guests were, as the French say, of an impeccable correctness. They were at ease, conversed of this and that, used the right forks, and asked for more olives. At my table were a professor of research histology, a railroad fireman, and a political lawyer. They seemed to have amiable interests in common, and drew me into conversation. Except that the lawyer believed Harding was still president, while the railroad fireman thought we were on a boat, their conversation was lucid and casual.

I felt awful, but not too awful yet. I managed to eat a little, and wondered if I were going to be kept awake all night again. When we arose from table, I asked Mr. Dirk if anything had been done about it. He said my room was being changed to a bigger one, more quiet, around the corner of the corridor. We all gravitated into the lobby. We found two young men whom I took to be patients already installed there, in wheel chairs, smoking cigarettes. They were not dressed and had evidently been fed in their bedrooms. They were the first two who looked and acted the way you had a right to expect patients to look and act in the sort of place this was. One was a beautiful youth with pale golden hair, in lavender Chinese pajamas embroidered with dragons. He giggled, invited Miss Pine to spank him severely, and said in a high, die-away voice like an actor imitating Noel Coward imitating a fairy, that Ezra Pound was abomination to little white cows. The other was a tough-looking foreigner with his head bandaged, face scratched, leg in splints—a sort of battlepiece, who sat and glowered savagely. Too dangerous, I figured, to be allowed to come to the dining room. As a matter of fact, he was a Magyar from the Carpathian mountains where they hunt bears with short daggers. He looked it. When he presently spoke—he seemed to be talking to Spike— he seemed to be growling something about the last time he told Mussolini something, and how many times you would be arrested if you went to California on a motorcycle in three days to the bedside of a dying wife who had sued you for running around with the one with red hair who used to be with a circus.

Spike was arguing with him, but didn't seem to be afraid of him. The other patients didn't seem to be afraid either. The political lawyer settled down to a pinochle game with Miss Pine, some others started a bridge game, several of them worked crossword puzzles in the evening papers. I guess Dirk saw me staring at the two madmen in wheel chairs for he said:

"Oh, by the way, you haven't met these two gentlemen of our staff, Mr. Heaney and Mr. Tiroschk. They work in another part of the hospital, but are on the sick list just now."

I thought of the Cabinet of Dr. Caligari. I wondered whether Dirk was kidding, or whether maybe Dirk was just plain crazy too. I was really puzzled and felt that I owed it to myself to do something about it. So I talked then and there, seriously, not about the weather, to Mr. Heaney and Mr. Tiroschk. Mr. Heaney said that about inviting Miss Pine to spank him, it was that he was getting over bronchitis, and that she and one of the doctors had told him just before dinner that he must stay in bed and not smoke cigarettes. As for Ezra Pound, he said that his mother had sent him the *Cantos* to read while he was sick and that everybody had been arguing about them and that he was merely continuing the argument. As for the little white cows, they were slang picked up from *South Wind* which his mother had sent him at the same time and which everybody had read too. About his imitating Noel Coward or a fairy, I refrained from asking. It wasn't necessary. He hadn't been imitating anybody. He talked that way naturally. Male nurses occasionally do. But not the bear-killer whom I tackled next. He was a tough hombre. He had been mixed up with Fascism in Rome in the castor oil days and had seen Mussolini plenty. He was a professional motorcycle racer—as well as an orderly just now on one of the violent "back halls"—and the number of times he had been arrested on the way to see his dying wife in California had been—believe it or not—nineteen. He had kept count of them. He had been pushing it up to as high as a hundred sometimes, he said, and sometimes they had telephoned to towns ahead to stop him. But the cops all let him go and helped him on his way, he said, when he showed them the telegram that his wife was dying. One cop in Iowa, he said, had paced him half way across the state. Several cops had paced him, he said, and he had made a record. As for the circus girl, he had met her while he was doing exhibition stunt riding, and you could hardly blame his poor wife, he said, who had been an invalid, for suing him and all that.

So everything was accounted for, including the invitation to spank, the little white cows, and the redheaded girl from the circus. They were not crazy. They were bonafide asylum employees. But it had bothered me. I had begun to wonder whether maybe Harding really was still president and whether I was maybe still on a boat, like the fireman. That is, I had begun to wonder whether my drinking hadn't been merely a plausible pretext used by my friends to put me in a place where I ought to be for an entirely different reason. During those first days, unless there was a white coat or uniform to go by, I found it practically impossible to guess which were patients and which were attendants. Even with the staff doctors, you simply had to learn their faces. There were numerous doctors of medicine, dentistry and divinity among the patients, so that when you were introduced to a new "doctor" you never knew by the mere title which side of the fence he might be on. You had to suspend judgment and draw your own conclusions, which you couldn't always sometimes do.

I was, however, certain about Dr. Hadden, the histologist, because I had sat with him at dinner. He was now playing bridge. I pulled a chair over near him. He was dealing. He said he didn't mind if I watched. He dealt himself a power house. He could have made an original two spade bid, forcing to game and perhaps to slam. He sorted his cards and passed listlessly. The other three passed, and the cards were thrown in. I asked him in undertones why he had done it. I was seeing everything acutely with a sort of puzzled fascination, but was still in a sort of detached, hangover haze.

"Because fate is against me," he whispered sadly, "I will explain it all to you one of these days and you will understand."

Another benevolent elderly gentleman who had finished his evening paper asked me how I liked everything, and when I told him, quite honestly, that I didn't know yet, he said he sincerely hoped I would be pleased, for they were sparing no expense; that it was now costing him nearly five million a year, and that he proposed installing a large swimming pool after Christmas.

The only noise in the big room was the pinochle game between Miss Pine and the lawyer who thought Harding was still president. They laughed and were gay together. I watched it for a little while. The lawyer was cheating flagrantly, and Miss Pine, instead of objecting, simply cheated more flagrantly on the sly.

He said to me, with a happy smile:

"You see, Miss Pine is the only person in the whole hospital who can give me a decent game. She can sometimes even beat me. The others play so poorly that I always beat them, and then they get jealous and accuse me of taking cards from the bottom."

He chuckled, Miss Pine melded four queens, and a gentleman asked me if I had read *Anthony Adverse*. His question made me realize that despite the strange fascination this new world had for me, I was in some curious way vaguely bored, vaguely disappointed. The truth is that I was beginning to have the curious "Is that all?" feeling from which I have suffered since the first time I went to a circus. I had it when I first heard Caruso sing and when I first went up in an airplane. It had followed me into deserts, jungles, devil-worship crypts in Kurdistan and voodoo temples. It was catching up with me again in this weird place. So I picked up a magazine. I picked up a copy of *Vanity Fair*. On its back cover was a color photograph of Mrs. Powell Cabot, poised, young and beautiful, endorsing a brand of cigarette. But the name of the lady, in big, clear type, had been carefully black-blocked with a heavy pencil so that it now read:

MRS. POEL CAT

I realized that this was not hilariously funny and not precisely in restrained good taste, but it somehow relieved my depression. Instead of feeling "Is that all?" I felt that it was quite enough for the first evening, and went to bed feeling that no matter how much the doctors decorated the hash with my mother's sprig of parsley, there was strong meat beneath the camouflage.

III

ON THE second day, the doctors started working on me. It was time. During the first night and day, I had been in a more or less aggressive alcoholic daze, at the same time fascinated and resentful toward my new surroundings, but now I was a wreck. For nearly two years I had been drinking a quart to a quart and a half of whiskey, brandy, gin or Pernod daily,[1] and now I had been without any for approximately thirty-six hours. They didn't try to get me out of bed. The morning cup of black coffee shook so that I spilled part of it, and I had to press my arms against my body to steady my hands, unbuttoning my pajamas when the first doctor came to prod my liver.

It was soon after breakfast. He stared at me with keen curiosity, told me his name was Paschall, and that he was to be my regular doctor. He had an open

[1] AUTHOR'S NOTE: This had been in France, where liquor is good, plentiful, and not expensive, but I doubt that the country, quality, brands, nature, or even *quantity* were material to my plight. Better men have survived more and worse liquor elsewhere.

face and looked like a straight-shooter. After thump-
ing me, taking my blood pressure, pulse and whatnot,
he asked me when I had come in, and when he saw me
getting angry he said, before I could say it:

"No, no, I know exactly when you came in. I'll be
asking you in a minute who brought you—I know that
too—and where you think you are. . . ."

"I'm sorry," I said, "I forgot. You have to see
whether I'm focusing or not."

"That's it," he said. "Are you?"

"I think so," I said. "I don't think it has affected
me that way. It's my nerves that are shot."

We soon found that they were shot to a degree
which I had automatically concealed from my friends
and myself. I was certain, for instance, that I could
sign my name and pick up a glass—which were about
the only two things I had been doing regularly since
the last Fourth of July and it was now nearly Christmas—but we discovered that to sign my name I had
to press my wrist, elbow, and whole hand flat against
the table, and that when I picked up a glass or anything I must always steady my elbows against my
ribs. When I shut my eyes and tried to touch my nose,
I missed my head. It scared me. Of course if I hadn't
been pretty seriously scared already, I would never

had had myself locked up, but now when he held a mirror and showed me that my mouth twitched, I was even more frightened, and thoroughly disgusted. I said:

"Jesus, so that's the way it is. Well, you've got to keep me locked up in this place if it takes . . ."

He said:

"Well, if that's the way you feel about it, we may be able to do you some good."

I said:

"Listen, doctor, I'd rather be dead than the way I am. That's why I'm here. I'll stand for anything. It's up to you."

He said:

"Well, then, in the first place, I'll tell you the worst. No tapering off."

I didn't say anything to that, and he continued:

"We can give you something to take the place of it at first, if we have to, but we'd rather not. We have other methods, which you probably won't like, but they're better."

I said:

"I told you it's up to you, and besides you've got me where it doesn't make any difference whether I like it or not. Haven't you?"

He grinned and said, "Oh, you've found that out, have you?"

I said, "Sure, Spike told me about it yesterday."

"Ever hear of prolonged baths?" he asked presently. I told him I'd heard of them, vaguely, for maniacs and girls in Bedford. "Yes," he said, "that's the idea. They quiet your nerves."

"Okay," I said. "My nerves need quieting."

So during the next few days I learned all about prolonged baths, and learned also—without smashing any of the furniture or trying to smash any of the attendants, which is the usual preliminary—everything about the mysterious "pack" which is the only method of prolonged physical restraint now regarded as cricket by modernized institutions which can swear without perjuring themselves that they have thrown all the straitjackets, handcuffs and muffs out of the window. "Pack" bears the same relation to "straitjacket" that "mental hospital" does to "insane asylum." It is up my sainted mother's alley. It is a rose by any other name. It is my dear, dead mother's liberty cabbage.

But I'd better tell first about the bath, which began

that morning and lasted more or less all day. A new male nurse named Diesel, that is, new to me . . . took me to a tiled room where there was an oversize bathtub. He lined it with sheets and got rubber pillows and stuffed my ears with oiled cotton and brought another armful of sheets but hesitated with them, looking at me.

He said, "You won't jump out, will you?"

I said, "I don't know. Will I?"

"Oh, well," he said, running the tub full of water, and arranging the sheets so I couldn't jump out. He adjusted the drain stopcock and turned the spiggots on so that the running water stayed on a level with my chin, dried his hands, tilted a chair, lighted a cigarette which was against the rules and pulled a copy of *Murder in the Rain* out of his pocket. He told me I could go to sleep if I wanted to, that he would keep an eye on me to see that my head didn't slide under.

Every quarter of an hour or so, he stuck a thermometer in the water. After a little while the water seemed (to me) to have no temperature whatever. That is, I no longer had any slightest sensation of warmth or coolness. It was like having no body, floating in an astral dream. My nerves were jangling, but

they were like wireless vibrations in the sense that they
didn't seem to be connected or grounded in material,
muscle or tissue. I told him about it, and he said it was
because the water was at blood heat, to a fraction. He
showed me the thermometer, taking pride in his trade.
He explained to me that there was also an electric
thermostat with double automatic valve control, so
that I ran no risk of scalding like the brave engineer,
no matter whether he and the fireman were careless or
not. "He was going down grade at ninety miles an
hour when his whistle began to scream," thought I, and
was comforted. He laid the detective story down and
we talked a little. He explained that Hall Four—
everything was called "hall" instead of ward—was
the reception hall, to which all patients were brought
when first admitted; that it was also the observation
hall to which patients were frequently sent back for a
day or for weeks; and that it was also the "sick" hall
for both patients and resident staff, which accounted
for the presence of Heaney and Tiroschk. He explained that the "numbers" of the halls were arbitrary,
that they had seemed "cuckoo" to him when he first
came, like the numbers in a crap game if you don't
know how to shoot crap. You came in on Four; if you
were violent, you went to Eight or Nine; if you stayed

there a long while, you might go to Five; and when you were calmed or nearly cured you went to Hall Two. It still seemed "cuckoo" to him, he said, the way halls were numbered.

The female patients? . . . Yes, they were under the same roof, but way over in an entirely different set of halls, nearly a quarter of a mile away. Yes, I'd see them all, or most of them, at church, the movies, dances. There were some good lookers too, he added. I thought I was learning a lot, though I hadn't really learned anything yet. It was a strange new world in which I was still a neophyte. It had its rituals—psychiatry sometimes seems crazier than any of the patients it treats. For instance, the ritual at the dances had to be experienced to be believed at all, and then you wondered how anybody could have invented it.

Diesel went back to his *Murder in the Rain.* I told him I had to have a cigarette. He said, well, we weren't supposed to smoke in here, but that I must feel pretty awful if I had been drinking as much as they said I had, and that I'd be there for a couple of hours more, so he fixed the sheets so that one of my hands could come through, and dried it, and lighted me one. Then I sort of went to sleep.

I felt just as jerky when he took me out and dried

me as I had been before it started, but he said it had
relaxed my tension some. The doctors, who had let me
alone the first day, now came around in droves, at intervals. I was back in my bedroom, in pajamas and
dressing gown, to make it easier for them. Dirk had
been given orders not to make me dress or go to the
dining room. They let me loll and wander from my
room to the smoking room or not, as I pleased. During
some of the time, all the other patients had disappeared from the hall. They were all somewhere else.
It was a bad, interminable day for me—though they
made it as easy as they could—wanting a drink so
badly that I wondered if I would have gulped Jamaica
ginger or even denatured alcohol. I decided that I
would. It had been time all right for me to be locked
up. But it was going to be tough.

That afternoon their non-resident diagnostician, a
doctor almost as famous as a movie star, came and
gave me a complete once-over. A half dozen of the
staff doctors drifted in, decently asking permission, to
watch the famous man and take notes. It appeared
that none of my organs was corroded, that I was just
a plain drunk with the jitters and a reasonable chance
of being cured, if there is any chance of a drunkard
ever being cured, which the French and Spanish do

not believe. The old Spanish proverb says, "There is
no cure for a drunkard but death," and the French
say, "*Qui a bu, boira*." The psychiatrists have invented
a new proverb almost as savage, if a little less hopeless, but we'll come to that later. Just now it was getting dark again, and I didn't feel that I could ever go
to sleep again—though previously I had been falling
into heavy stupors easily—unless they gave me drink
or dope.

My nerves were jangling like cracked fire alarms.

When Paschall came around that night and saw I
really needed a dope-pill or a triple bromide, he said,
"I'll leave an order so you can get it if you think you
must, but there's a way we think is better. It may not
work with you. You may lose your temper. But we
might try it. Want to try it?"

"Yes, what?" I said. "Try anything."

He went away and pretty soon the prize-fighter and
another husky came in, carrying what looked like the
hotel wet-wash. They fixed the bed so it wouldn't soak
through to the mattress, then laid me straight and
naked on the bed with my arms pressed along my sides
like a soldier lying at attention and began swathing
me, rolling me on one side and then the other, in tight
wet sheets, so that the weight of my body rolling back

would pull them smoother and tighter, over and over
again, until they stood off to smooth any wrinkles out
of the job and look at it and see if it was all right. I
was flat on my back. Except that my head stuck out
and lay comfortably on a pillow, I was the mummy of
Rameses. I couldn't bend my elbows or knees. I
couldn't even double my fists. My hands were pressed
flat. I couldn't move a muscle except by telegraphing
a deliberate local order to it as oriental dancers do.
This was the famous "pack." It occurred to me that
I'd have been willing to bet any amount of money—
and I still would—that this would have held Houdini.
I had seen straitjackets on the vaudeville stage, and
a straitjacket was a ten-acre field compared to this
cocoon. It was tighter than any kid glove. And the
tightness was so uniform that it didn't stop circulation.
After they had gone I started to get excited locally,
and it stopped even that. They told me I'd sweat a lot
presently, and had fixed an ice pack on the top of my
head where the skull was thickest. They had turned
out all the lights, but had left the door slightly ajar,
and had told me that they'd be down the hall somewhere so that if anything went wrong I could let out
a yell.

I lay there in the darkness like an Egyptian

mummy. After a while my mind began to work, and I
discovered that I liked it. It occurred to me that probably I was masochistic or something of the sort. I set
about rationalizing it, but of course one always does.
I remembered the theories that we all have a subconscious longing to be back in the womb—that we remember subconsciously how nice and safe and warm it
was. I remembered poetry about the womb and the
grave. There were some distant, ordinary, living,
human sounds way down the corridor somewhere, but
they didn't disturb or concern me. Perhaps they did
disturb me, for I became acutely conscious again of
my jangled nerves. I wanted to turn over, to "toss"
about in the bed. I wanted to put my elbow up under
the pillow. I wanted to move my arms. I wanted to
scratch my forehead. I'd have to yell for help if a fly
alighted on my nose. In a little while, the active nervousness decreased, but I was conscious of increasing
tension. I tried experimentally to break, or stretch my
bonds, by contracting and straining every muscle. I
found that I couldn't loosen them at all, and it was
this that had excited me and made me like it. I went
lax presently and was beginning to sweat. I sweated,
time passed, and the tension was gone and the jangling
nervousness disappeared too, faded slowly as it does

under a strong soporific. I was soon as peaceful as a four-month fetus.

When they came back after a long time and began to unwind me, I was still peaceful. And when they went away I turned on my side, stuck my arm up under my head, and went to sleep without another movement.

I was put to bed that way for five or six successive nights, and then Dr. Paschall ordered it stopped. He said I liked it too well—that it could get to be another habit, like dope, veronal or whiskey, and advised me to read *La Sequestrée de Poitiers.*

IV

OWARD the end of a week they began to merge
me into the group, to cog me in with the Hall
Four machinery. I mean, special things stopped
happening to me; they stopped shunting and dragging
me from hell to breakfast for special examinations,
treatments, wrappings, tappings; they began to make
me do the same things everybody else did. They made
me a member of the kindergarten, took me for walks
with the rest of the class, gave me work to do and
things to play with.

There were fourteen of us on Hall Four then, semi-
permanent on that hall, while the doctors were making
up their minds where each of us should be subsequently
quartered—in one of the howling back-halls under
constant observation, or in one of the "villas" where
you had almost as much freedom as in a summer
boarding house or sanitarium-hotel. There is something
I had better try to explain at this point,—if the general picture is to make sense. I was an alcoholic, but I

was not now, or at any time thereafter, put with a group of other alcoholics. The groupings were on a different basis. Take the fourteen of us, for instance, who were grouped together in this intermediate hall. Our ailments were quite dissimilar, just as ailments are, for example, in a surgical ward or the accident ward of a regular hospital, where one man has appendicitis, and another hernia or mastoiditis; where one has broken his arm falling off a ladder, while the man in the bed next to him has been slashed in a fight or cracked on his head in an automobile smash-up. So it was here. One of us had melancholia, another suffered from hallucinations, so-and-so was elated, another was manic-depressive, still another, who seemed completely sane, was with us solely because he had occasional uncontrollable impulses to jump out of high windows or in front of motor busses. Our only similarity was that our various ailments were in the stage or tempo which made the tempo of this hall the right one temporarily for our treatment and observation. I was the only alcoholic in the group. There were only a few drunks, indeed, in the whole place, a scattering half dozen, maybe, among three hundred patients. As a matter of fact, while they accept patients in this category and sometimes cure them, they are not very keen on taking

them. They don't like to take cases which they may
not be able to cure, and, contrary to some impressions,
the whiskey habit is harder to cure than the general
run of ordinary mental derangements.

While our ailments were dissimilar, as I say, there
was one respect in which we were all alike—one thing
which differentiated us from people on the outside,
made it expedient for us to be locked up. I soon had
this figured out. It is no illuminating contribution on
my part to psychiatry. But it helps paint the picture.
I figured it out for myself. It checked on all of us. It
clicked on each diversified one of us, including myself.
It negated, incidentally, the Pirandello-ish notion,
widely prevalent, that "if the truth were known,"
nine-tenths of all the people of your acquaintance
. . . including perhaps yourself . . . are "outside"
only because you haven't been "caught" as it were.
When my friend, C— B—, the modernist painter,
came, full of curiosity to see me, and met some of my
fellow-inmates, he said:

"Hell, the whole gang that comes to my studio Saturday nights belongs in a hatch a damned sight more
than you or any of these fellows. We're all soaked
with gin and as crazy as bats. You're taking a rest-
cure, you bum!"

And my friend, Professor T—, who has an international reputation as a philosopher, with a chair in one of the major universities, confessed that he always felt a sense of embarrassment, of furtiveness, of guilt, when he came to see me. He was afraid, he said, they'd "find out" and keep him there.

Well, that prevalent Pirandello notion, which I used to have myself, is wrong and I can prove it. I can prove it by the one criterion that clicked, checked, on all of us locked up in there, and that would not click, check, on the painter, the professor, or any of the rest of you who were going about your business free on the outside:

Take young Hauser, our youngest, a favorite on the hall, a brilliant, amusing chap—up to a certain point. He was "elated." He sparkled. He had finished, precociously, his academic course at Princeton with honors, including the Phi Beta Kappa key at nineteen, and was headed toward the medical school when his father, who was a doctor, had sent him here to the nut school instead. He did Bob Benchley stuff. The difference between him and Benchley, was that Benchley controlled the stuff. Benchley rode it. Hauser couldn't control it. He did it whether he wanted to or not. He did it when he didn't want to. It rode him. He couldn't control it.

Take my morose friend, Papa Renwick. He was the
diametric opposite of Hauser. He was so melancholy
that he wanted to die. Lots of people on the outside
are so melancholy they want to die. But they control
it. They don't try several times to jump out windows
as Papa Renwick had done. He couldn't control it.

Take young Frainer. His case was a queer one. He
is cured now, I've heard. But it took longer to cure
him than it did some who were brought in howling or
imagining they were ancient emperors. Yet he seemed
to have absolutely nothing the matter with him except
that he was a pain in the neck to everybody and
seemed to need a good clout on the jaw more than he
did psychiatric treatment. His appearance was against
him. He had a head like Byron or Apollo, and the sort
of nip-waisted, long-limbed, flat-flanked, beautifully
shouldered body that made any clothes he put on look
as if they had come from the Prince of Wales' private
tailor. He had an authentic Boston Back Bay accent
which made even Miss Pine and the doctors feel in-
ferior, and the manners of Lord Godalmighty. He
had, on top of all this, an aggressive superciliousness
and selfishness which were painful and astounding. As
when he let the crate of fruit his family sent him rot
rather than give any of us an orange. There was nothing else mental or moral the matter with him. But

this one thing had been enough. His unpopularity—to use a mild word for it—in the outside world had become as super as his superciliousness. He had been asked to leave a succession of banks and brokerage offices in which his influential family had placed him; his fiancée had thrown him over in disgust; servants, waiters, taxi drivers, clerks in stores invariably wanted to kill him, and no young women, or men either, of his own set could abide him. His parents, even his mother, had the extraordinary sense to see that the fault was with him, and that if he weren't cured of it, life would junk him. Honest medical psychologists consulted by his parents had guessed that the real young man, overlaid with all this, was a sweet-natured, rather timid, decent chap, but that it would take a year or more in some psychiatric institution where he would "get the works," to break through the overlay and cure him. So here he was in our midst. Why? Not because he was supercilious and super-selfish. You know plenty of people like that outside who are often successful, if not beloved. They use it as armor and as a weapon. Using it, they control it. But this poor fellow had it as a disease, like jaundice or measles. He couldn't control it.

Then there was Professor Jeffries, the mathematician. His mind raced. He played with primes. Cube roots cluttered his brain and whirled in it. Controlling the clutter, he had been a brilliant teacher and a "lightning calculator" as well, using this latter freak-ish talent merely to amuse himself or private friends, since he didn't have to commercialize it. Now he had lost control of it. It controlled him. He was harmless, but had to be watched all the time. Undressed for bed and in his pajamas, he forgot one night to get in the bed and when the night watchman's light flashed through the open door hours later, he was standing absorbed in the middle of the room. His racing mathe-matical mind, controlled, had been in a fair way to make him famous. Uncontrolled, it had put him here.

Take my friend Spike. Women were his trouble. For years he had obeyed that impulse, or tried to, with every pretty female he met. Enthusiastic, capable, a Don Juan in the rough, women fell for him. Men liked him too . . . kidded him . . . admired his speed and technique—until something short-circuited in Spike's cortex. His speed accelerated, but he lost his control and technique entirely. He began leaping on pretty girls, leaping like the baboon in the limerick on the banks of the Ganges where the sacred maidens congregate to swim. So here he was in our kindergarten. I suppose all males have the leaping impulse occasionally, on Fifth Avenue in May, or in a ballroom, but we generally control it, or at least say, "Haven't I met you somewhere?" and, "Let's have a quiet cocktail at Pierre's . . ." before we leap. They had kept Spike for a while on the back halls, like the ape he was, but he had made progress. He could now look at Miss Pine without leaping, just as in a few months I would be able to look at a bottle labeled Johnny Walker without grabbing it and trying to guzzle it. But it wouldn't be safe for a long time to turn me loose in a bar-room or Spike on a bathing beach.

So, take me now, in turn, as a case like the others. For many previous years I had been drinking, sometimes a lot, when I wanted to, getting tight intentionally and liking it, sobering up when I wanted to, or thought I ought to, and staying sober for long periods to grind out quantities of work. I know plenty of good citizens, business men, artists, writers, who not only go in heavily for highballs and cocktails, but get cockeyed, cooked to the crow's nest, whenever they choose —which is pretty often with some of my friends on both sides of the Atlantic—and who nevertheless, year after year, keep their health and balance, do their work, turn out distinguished product in good volume.

I know now that being soused frequently, being half cock-eyed half the time, passing out at parties, being put to bed by the taxi driver or fighting with policemen, isn't being a drunkard. So long as any man drinks when he wants to and stops when he wants to, he isn't a drunkard, no matter how much he drinks or how often he falls under the table. The British upper classes were constantly and consistently mildly stewed, from father to son, in Parliament and Pall Mall for nearly the whole of the eighteenth century. It isn't drinking that makes a drunkard. I had drunk for years, enthusiastically, and with pleasure, when I wanted to. Then something snapped in me, and I lost control. I began to have to have it when I didn't want it. I couldn't stop when I wanted to. Instead of being a pleasure any more, it was just too bad. I wasn't here because I drank a lot . . . or too much. I was here, just like the rest, because I had lost control.

Of course there were others of us whose loss of control was more diffuse, less easy to define—the paranoiacs, schizophrenics, catatonics, the ones who had elaborate hallucinations, the manic-depressives, and my other friend and later buddy, Charlie Logan, the human barometer, who howled like a wolf whenever the weather was changing. Despite the common denominator, we had a kaleidoscopic divergence of cases.

So here I was, an inmate of this extraordinary locked-and-barred kindergarten, for the same good reason as the rest. We were a bunch of grown men, most of us mature, who had lost control of ourselves in one way or another and who had to be controlled by others . . . that is, treated like a bunch of children . . . that is, put back in the nursery.

The longer I stayed there, the more I saw and experienced, the more it seemed to me, often fantastically, to be a kindergarten or a nursery. Despite court commitments, despite bars and huskies, it was more like a nursery than a prison.

I was shut up in this queer place for seven long months, authentically as one of them, needing restraint and treatment as badly as any of the rest, yet different in the one respect, that at no time after my hang-over daze had cleared up was I mentally clouded or twisted. I was not a "mental case." My chart read "psychopathic symptoms, zero." In short—though I belonged there—since they had enlarged their function to include the care and treatment of inebriates—I was nevertheless in a situation which gave me a somewhat special opportunity to see, experience, be an intimate part of, a strange world whose intimate customs and rituals are surrounded with mystery, misapprehension, and some fear, since it is a world closed generally to any save its doctors and employees on the one hand, its psychopathically deranged patients on the other. I saw it with clear eyes, and am writing about it with no prejudice—no real purpose, even, beyond that of hoping to do a good piece of reporting. I am not aiming to expose, attack or praise the queer place, to paint it red, or black, or white. I am aiming to paint it as it was. It had plenty of color of its own. It had every tone of the spectrum.

And one of its permanent, dominant overtones was this back-to-childhood, back-to-the-kindergarten element. We were handled as children—not as delinquent or bad children, necessarily—but, rather, as potentially decent, irresponsible children who didn't know what was good for us, and therefore frequently had to be told. It was a "mamma knows best" or "teacher knows best" atmosphere, protective and generally kindly, but backed up with "mamma will spank" when children became unmanageable and just had to be dragged kicking to bed without their suppers. Dirk's making me brush my hair whether I wanted to or not, then beaming blandly, seemed to be the essence of it. What gave it sometimes a crazy-dream quality—quite apart from the fact that some of us were crazy—was the fact that all of us were grown men, many of us middle-aged or elderly men of the type which generally bosses and orders other people around in the outside world. To the casual eye, we were well dressed, responsible, mature, none of us physical invalids. When our nurse, Miss Pine, took us to walk, we looked like a delegation of prominent Rotarians. We rambled about a good deal, both in the buildings and snow-covered park, nearly always in sole charge of Miss Pine! We grown men went to play in the snow in charge of a young girl in nurse's uniform who scolded us if we forgot our rubbers and told us when we had to go back indoors. Sometimes one of the huskies was off somewhere in the background when we went out, but usually not. When we returned, Miss Pine saw to it that we put on dry socks before going to supper if we'd got our feet wet, and made the political lawyer eat all his spinach before he could have his pie. She made old Mr. Wylie take his mineral oil whether he wanted to or not, and her methods of persuasion were identical with those used with temperamental children. She sometimes even shook us, or slapped us, or threatened to, though this of course was against all rules, and she did it only as a sort of joke and only to patients she liked.

Four days a week, she took us to the barber shop, through the long corridors, unlocking the doors, counting us, and bringing up the rear. Often there was something sad, almost sinister, about that special procession. We usually walked single file, not that there was any rule about it, but in one of the long, bare connecting corridors there was a narrow strip, a "runner" I believe it is called, and we got the habit of walking single file on it. Not all the patients were always cheerful, and early morning is never a very gay time in any sort of an institution, so that often most of them walked silently with their heads down. I was a part of it myself. Yet I could see it. One of the depressed ones, leaving, cured, months later, told me that he remembered those walks to the barber shop as the most horrible experience of his life. Back in December, the time of which I am now writing, one could never have guessed that he was noticing anything. He was like an automaton. He walked with the rest of us like an automaton. We all, as well as Miss Pine, looked after him a little—prevented him from walking on in a straight line when there was a corner to turn—made him sit down when it was time to sit down. He seemed oblivious as a robot. Yet he told me afterward that those walks to the barber shop had filled him always with horror. He had believed then, he said, that he would *walk in a line of men like that, somewhere, silent and single file, all the rest of his life.*

But such things were the secret undertones. Superficially—and generally factually too for the most of us—we all seemed a bunch of worried business men with a morning grouch going to the barber shop. When we got there, we brightened up, smoked cigarettes, read the morning papers, argued about the NRA and kidded Eddie. We were generally a cheerful nursery, and liked our pretty nurse. We were a cheerful kindergarten and liked our pretty teacher.

We talked about it sometimes among ourselves, got a kick out of it, knew it was pleasant. No responsibilities, no obligations, no problems to meet or solve, no duties or decisions. We didn't even have to decide when to get up in the morning or when to go to bed. Somebody else looked after us. Somebody else looked after everything. Lots of us had been grown-up and responsible, meeting worries, problems, obligations, for twenty, thirty years. So that cured now, on the outside, where I have to decide everything for myself, I remember the haven it was . . . almost wish sometimes I were back there, back in the arms of my nut-college mother.

How dear to my heart are the scenes of my child-

hood, when fond recollection recalls them to view—or
when things get too hot for fiddlers. Turn backward,
turn backward, O time, in your flight and make me a
child again just for tonight. I've heard bearded
Frenchmen sobbing, "*Maman, maman, maman!*" shot
through the guts in the barbed wire entanglements,
and once heard a man bleat it standing on a wooden
platform just before the sheriff sprung the trap. When
life gets too hot, we want to go back. Life had gotten
too hot for us. That's why we were back in a nursery.

I knew it was good for me. I suppose I was one of
the good boys in the nursery—which was a new rôle
for me. But we had bad boys too on our hall, some of
whom I was afraid of until I got to know them better.
There was one bad boy with big mustaches named
Giasconti. I remember him vividly. I hadn't talked
with him the first week, and didn't know how bad he
was. He was thin, hollow-cheeked, with jet-black,
straight hair, and smooth, waxen, olive skin. He
seldom spoke, and never read the newspapers. He had
a little weaver's frame with shuttles, which he rested
on his knee and worked at in the evening. Dirk had
told me he was a coffee merchant, and I guessed that
he might be of South American origin.

One evening, I admired the bright scarf he was

weaving, and asked him if the design were Spanish.
He stopped weaving, sat motionless as a statue, and
said in an earnest, low, unhurried voice, with his face
expressionless as a mask:

"You son of a bitch, you fairy, you pervert; you
child-raper; you filth, you scum, you swine; I'll shoot
you, I'll hang you, I'll kill you, I'll drown you, I'll
cut your heart out with a dull knife."

Before I could blink or say boo, he dropped his eyes
and calmly resumed his weaving. Two attendants
materialized, close, as if by magic, though no voice
had been raised, and nothing happened. His idiosyncrasy was explained to me. The words "Spaniard" and
"Spanish" were his specialty. He had the foreign look.
You could ask him if he were an Italian, Greek, or
even a Turk, and he would reply with smiling cour-
tesy. But if you suggested that Velasquez, or a bull-
fight, or an onion were Spanish, he deemed it a deadly
personal insult. He was quite harmless—or he
wouldn't have been on Hall Four—and believed that
Miss Pine was secretly in love with him.

Having tried to describe the patients of our hall as
a general group, and having tried to convey an idea of
the dominant atmosphere of the place, I suppose it is
time now to round out the general outline of the picture by describing one of our days:

We were awakened at seven, had showers and dressed, had breakfast at quarter to eight, during which at least one of the staff doctors came through on his rounds. The ritual was prescribed and unwavering. We went on eating, but he had to say "Good morning" to each of us by name, adding "How do you feel this morning?" or "Did you sleep all right?" or "Is the coffee all right?" or "Is everything all right?" and had to listen patiently—within reasonable limits —to what each of us had to say in return. After breakfast, we smoked and read the morning papers in the library, watching the tall, grandfather clock, until at exactly half past eight a puffy little man who seemed always to be wearing a derby hat even when he removed it, let himself in from the outside with a passkey, stood in his overcoat, and said in a nasal voice which he tried to inflect with a crooning maternal caress:

"OCCU-PAY-SHUN!"

Whereupon Dirk, Gilmore, the male nurses, Miss Pine buzzed around, helping us into our overcoats, finding our rubbers and galoshes, counting noses, rounding up Mr. Wylie, who sometimes hid under his bed and once in a wardrobe.

All bundled and counted, out we went into the snow, shepherded by the little man in the derby. The

Occupation Building was some hundreds of yards distant in the park, through the trees, on a rise, reached by a winding concrete path kept generally clean of snow by the "outdoor squad" which consisted of patients who chose it by preference, along with one or two who were forced to work outdoors by the doctors' orders and didn't like it at all. Pavlovitz, a boisterous, red-cheeked popular Russian Jew who had made a fortune in wholesale hardware and then gone haywire, usually shouted greetings and took a shot at the derby with a hunk of snow. Fred Rau, a thin, nervous, melancholy public accountant, plucked at our sleeves as we passed, and muttered:

"They can't leave us out here to die in the storm!"

Inside the locked door of the Occupation Building, its superintendent lurked waiting for us. He was a man with oyster-colored teeth, iron-gray hair to match, and chronic indigestion. It was just as the Listerine advertisements tell you. He was conscientious and probably had a kind heart. But nobody loved him.

The entrance hall was a museum, with glass cases, a hodge-podge of handicraft done by former patients —a great deal of it in the most godawful Victorian, Elbert Hubbard style, since all *art moderne* was discouraged—but done with a technical skill not to be sneezed at. The institution made it a point, I think, to discourage the sort of originality which is encouraged in modern art schools outside. It was all very well for Mrs. Whitney and the Independents to exhibit a stone egg as a portrait of a lady, but it was deemed better, on the whole, for us not to do crazy stuff, since most of us were really crazy. When Phillip Reed, who worked in plaster, did an amazing frieze of penguins which did not remotely resemble penguins but might have won a prize in any outside modernistic salon, Mr. Purdy put him to studying St. Gaudens and Rosa Bonheur. When Hauser, in the draught-room, invented a hexagonal chessboard to be played on simultaneously by four people, with green and orange pieces as well as red and black ones, he was transferred hastily to the department in which old gentlemen put bristles in scrubbing brushes which were all of a soothing similarity.

Within what they regarded as reason, however, patients were permitted to adopt the occupation which individually pleased them best, and we had a pretty wide choice. There were departments of basketry, weaving, brush-making, book-binding, printing, metal work, carpentry, leather, the graphic and plastic arts. Of course many of these crafts involved the use of pointed or edged tools, not to mention the "dull, blunt instruments" dear to coroners' juries, and new patients who might be dangerous to themselves or others were generally put for a while in basketry until they could be sized up.

They had sent me to the basketry room, with an alternate choice of the brush room, but I had rebelled, and my doctor, Paschall, who was, as I have said, a good scout and a straight shooter, smoothed it for me. I had told him that it would make me think of Oscar Wilde picking oakum and be bad for my morale. So they let me go straight into carpentry, which was unusual. I liked it fine. The shop was in charge of an English master carpenter from Leeds named Joseph Byne, and was equipped with standard benches, ample tools, power lathe—everything a regular shop should have, plus the able instructions of Joseph. With a good log of seasoned white oak [1] and a set of drawings, I went to work to make a solid chair and table, morticed and joined solidly. I am as proud of them as of any writing I have ever done. They will probably last longer.

---

[1] AUTHOR'S NOTE: I promised "Dr. Storm" I would mention that the hardwood used in our carpentry and cabinet work is from trees grown on the place, felled, trimmed, and seasoned *by patients*. He is very proud of this.

Arriving each morning at the Occupation Building, our Hall Four kindergarten scattered to the various departments, where we met and worked with patients who had come from other halls. But we never saw women here. They had a separate Occupation Building of their own. We worked from about quarter to nine until eleven, when a whistle blew. We assembled in the hall and were re-sorted, after which we were marched, by group, out through the snow again, to the gymnasium, which was a couple of hundred yards distant, on the other side of the hill. On this excursion we were shepherded by Timothy Devlin, the elderly physical director who had been a friend of Muldoon's, and three or four of his young gymnasium assistants. They liked their jobs, and generally liked us. There was more fun in it, "more variety," Tim confided to me later, than working in an ordinary club or training camp.

The gymnasium had bowling alleys, billiards, pool, and ping-pong in the basement, marble-tiled locker room with showers; a spacious, armory-like cage above for indoor tennis, volley ball, basket ball and running.

Here again we mixed with patients from the other halls, including some of the wild men, howlers and humming birds from the back halls, who frequently

contributed the "variety," which kept Timothy's life
from being humdrum. And here again we were encouraged—within reason—to choose the games or exercise
which pleased us individually. Those who were elderly
or in bad physical shape, played bowls or billiards.
Those who felt more strenuous engaged in the group
games upstairs. I bowled a few mornings, then went
upstairs to watch the volley ball, and afterward
played on one of the teams. The first morning I went
up as a spectator, a little dentist named Dr. Stelzer
was creating a diversion. He was generally a good
player, they said, a good man to choose in picking a
winning team, but this morning, whenever the ball
came near him, instead of sending it back over the net,
he would hit it angrily with the full force of his fist,
so that it went off at any and all angles, out of bounds,
up in Mabel's room, or into the midriff of a teammate
who hadn't dodged in time. Each time he did it, Stelzer grimaced ferociously.

Timothy, who had his own way of handling us,
called a halt, and said:

"Listen, Dr. Stelzer, I want you to be more nonchalant."

Whereupon, Dr. Stelzer, taking the center of the
floor, forgetting all about whatever reasons he may
have had for his ferocity, embarked upon a philologi-

cal Socratic inquiry which presently involved Timothy
Devlin and most of the rest of us, as to just what the
word "nonchalant" really signified; as to whether
Timothy had used it correctly in meaning what Dr.
Stelzer took him to mean, and as to how one could tell
with certainty whether a person were being nonchalant
or not in a given circumstance. He proposed, I remember, that Timothy do certain unmentionable things
nonchalantly, and then "not nonchalantly."

By this time it was nearly noon, so the volley ball
game was abandoned, and we went to the showers.
We had a good time in the gymnasium. I have often
wondered what the psychiatric doctors would have
thought of it. Maybe Timothy told them, and maybe
he didn't.

At about quarter past twelve each day, sorted out
again, and in our own groups, we were taken back
from the gymnasium to our respective halls, and at
half past twelve, nearly always on the dot, we had
dinner. We dined in the middle of the day, instead
of in the evening—another thing most of us had rarely
done since childhood.

The food was good—for an institution. It was not
so good as the Ritz or Lafayette, but it was better than
most hospitals.

We were discouraged, after dinner, from taking

long postprandial naps—discouraged more particularly, though not absolutely forbidden, from flopping down on our beds. But in the smoking room and corridors were vast armchairs and vaster leather sofas, on which brief snoozing was winked at if one didn't abuse the privilege.

Toward half past three, or sometimes four, unless there was a raging storm, Miss Pine took us out again for an airing. If it were merely snowing heavily, or merely a crisp ten degrees below zero, out we went, protesting loudly that we'd perish, but enjoying it really. We took brisk walks round a quarter-mile circle, sometimes built snow men or snowball forts. We passed other groups of patients, including groups of occasional men from the back halls, but there wasn't much fraternizing in the cold. When spring and summer came, transforming the grounds into green lawns, groves and vistas, with a baseball diamond, tennis courts, bright-colored deck chairs strewn about, we mingled like the "happy family" which zoos and amusement resorts featured in the gay nineties— baboons, bears, bunnies and barnyard fowl, a calf and a couple of monkeys, with maybe a pig and a panther —all fenced in the same enclosure, living in more or less harmony, and making the feathers fly only occasionally.

Toward five o'clock in winter, with darkness falling, we went back to our hall in a glow, and at the ungodly (for grown-ups) hour of quarter past five, we had supper! For years I'd been dining at nearer eight, with supper, if any, toward midnight or one o'clock in the morning.

After supper, we generally played games, chess, checkers, dominoes and bridge in which Miss Pine occasionally joined us when she could be pried loose from pinochle with the perky little lawyer. She played a wild, crooked game—it would have been pointless for her to stick to Culbertson when she never knew what astronomical system, if any, her partner might be playing. She sometimes bid diamonds with a blank or a singleton, and then slid into spades which she held long with the tops. Smart and beautiful young women with a sense of humor can get away with murder anywhere—even in a booby kursaal.

At seven she disappeared, having been on and off duty for some twelve hours—as did our friends Dirk and Gilmore. The night force took over, including an elderly, virginal elephant with over-developed maternal instincts, who gave us milk and tucked us in bed. We drank the milk at half past eight, and nine o'clock was curfew. Back to childhood again. We were sent to bed at nine o'clock. Ten hours' sleep, instead of seven or eight, was supposed to be good for what ailed us. We got up at seven next morning, and that was our day round the clock in this modern, model "mental hospital" for which the doctors feel "asylum" is already an archaic and misleading word.

One regular, routine phase of it I've left out, which was intermittent, individual. More or less every day, at various times, as it could be most conveniently fitted into the schedules, we had hydrotherapy, massage, and brief naked sessions in the artificial sunlight room. More or less every day, too, we all had brief, private sessions, mostly talk, with our individual doctors.

V

LEST I have been painting the place too much as a paradise, it may be well now to introduce the fly in the ointment, the villain.

It wasn't the pot-bellied, bearded one, oozing authority. This Pot Belly, superintendent-general, turned out when you got to know him to be human. It wasn't the supreme head either, the president, Dr. Storm, who was remote like God, and hard to see.

The villain—that is of my piece—was a gentleman who came around at least once every day, a skinny, prim, nosy little gentleman with gold-rimmed spectacles, who was the superintendent-manager of the men's side of the institution. His name was Dr. Quigley. He was a psychiatrist, of course, but his job here was more of the floorwalker-managerial type, equipped with petty but sufficient delegated authority over the patients and attendants alike. So that he was more manager, more supervising boss than doctor, and the nature of his job was such that he would perhaps inevitably have been unpopular.

He was, as a matter of fact, pretty generally un-popular, but the mutual antipathy which arose and grew between him and me was a personal matter, and everything I tell about him will be, of course, preju-diced. I am writing about a man whom I didn't like, and who didn't like me. It is consequently impossible to expect me to be fair.

It began about prunes. But it had further conse-quences. As I have said, the food was good, and I am not very fussy about food anyway. It might not have happened. I got caught in it, and I think he did too. I had begun to notice that Perkins, who sat next to me at table, often had prunes, and that I never had. They were large, plump, swam in juice with fragments of lemon peel, and were sprinkled with cinnamon. He let me taste one, and I told Mr. Dirk that I would like to have prunes occasionally too. He said all right, but that I'd better just speak to Paschall, my doctor, about it.

"Sure, I'll fix it for you," said Paschall. "Prunes are supposed to be a part of the laxative diet, but that's all right, I'll fix it."

The next day, Perkins had prunes again, and I didn't. I supposed Paschall had forgotten so trivial a matter, and in a day or two, making no point of it, I mentioned it casually again. Paschall, to my surprise, looked embarrassed. "No, I never forget anything," he said. "The fact is Dr. Quigley doesn't think you should have them."

I looked at him, mystified. "You mean he thinks they would hurt me? Why, there's nothing the matter with my bowels, never has been."

"Yes, but that's just it," said Paschall. "Prunes list as laxative in the diet kitchen, and the point is that they're not supposed to be put on a patient's menu unless he needs them." He defended Quigley's point of view a little. He said it was a trivial matter in itself, but went against the rules, the system; that there had to be a system in a big place like this.

"You couldn't order them for me, as my doctor?" I asked.

"Not unless you're constipated," he grinned.

"Well, that's easy," I said. I wasn't sore—yet. But I thought it was silly—like big business "efficiency-expert" silliness—so I decided to have some fun with it, and, incidentally, to get the prunes.

It turned out not to be so easy. My first puerile plan was a fizzle. Every evening an attendant came around with the hall chart and a pencil, and asked each of us in a low, confidential voice, and we said yes or no as the case might be. Well, for five successive days I said "No." Meanwhile, at each meal, I waited, with decreasing confidence, for the prunes which never came, and finally said to Dirk:

"Don't the damned doctors ever look at our charts? Don't they know I'm in a bad way?"

He said:

"Don't kid yourself. If you try to kid the doctors, you're only kidding yourself, you know. Dr. Quigley's on to you. You're lucky he didn't put castor oil on your chart and make you take it."

I tried again to persuade Paschall. He said:

"You can't expect me to make a row about anything as silly as prunes. You ought to be ashamed of yourself."

"Is that so?" I said. "Well, maybe I can make a row."

The thing they're always most afraid of—next to suicide—is fire, even though the dump is 18-carat fireproof. I wrote a friend, and on Friday the friend brought me a pound of raw prunes. It violated no rules —visitors brought in fruit of all sorts—but when Dirk discovered what I had in the sack, he wanted to know what I was going to do with raw prunes.

I announced loudly that unless I was given cooked prunes at meals, I was going to break up the furniture, make a campfire in the middle of my bedroom, and cook these.

Some of my fellow-playmates thought it was funny, but Dirk didn't think it was funny at all. He picked up the house phone and broadcasted an S O S for Paschall, who appeared presently, took me round to my room, shut the door and said:

"Look here! Every time we've taken a drunk in this place, we've regretted it. I'll admit I thought maybe we'd get a different break with you. We've tried to give you a break, but I put it up to you. Don't you know we've got enough worry on our hands with real patients without your pulling a fake brainstorm like this?"

I said:

"Maybe you're mistaken. Maybe I've got a pathological craving for stewed prunes, like the pregnant woman who ate you-know-what."

He said:

"Say, don't pull that stuff! You're ham-acting. What you need is . . . If I had you on the outside . . ."

"You would, like hell," I said; "you can't even beat me at tennis—not outdoors. The light in the gymnasium bothered my eyes."

"I can beat you at Forest Hills, you soak, three sets out of five for any bet you like."

We talked about tennis a little, and then got back

to the prunes. I said I'd cook them on the tiles in the lavatory, where it couldn't set fire to any woodwork and could be cleaned up easily afterward. He said Quigley hadn't seen enough of me to know that I wasn't maybe really bughouse, maybe really turning dangerous with liquor taken away from me. I'd not only get myself thrown in with the real "wild ones" on one of the "back halls," he said, but would delay my own progress and perhaps be months in getting back to one of the front halls again.

I thought that over, and decided he was right. That night I had a private talk with Spike. He'd been in the place long enough to know just what sort of murder you might get away with, and what sort you couldn't. He said:

"Well, about the only tip I can give you is that they never penalize talk in this man's place. If you try to do anything, you get done in the eye, but sometimes you can wear them down with talk."

The next time Dr. Quigley came around—it happened to be at breakfast—routinely reached me, looked at me coldly through his gold-rimmed spectacles, and said perfunctorily, "Good-morning-how-are-you-Mr.-Seabrook," I got my lungs full of breath and said loudly:

"I'm not dying of chronic constipation *yet*, but the only reason is that for forty years I've eaten prunes, and now that I've been deprived of them in this prison I feel worse every day, and soon I'll probably be suffering from scurvy. I'm already developing pellagra, and . . ."

I had to pause because I had run out of breath. Dr. Quigley stared at me without replying, and moved coldly away. I wasn't discouraged. This was only a start. Dirk and the attendants didn't mind. They were beginning to be interested. Every time Quigley came near me for the next week or ten days, and every time I spied him within earshot no matter how inopportune the occasion, I aired my grievance loudly. I lay awake at night inventing variations, and borrowed a book about shipwrecked sailing vessels from which I cribbed painful accounts of what happened to sailors forced to live on salt pork and hardtack. Except for annoying Quigley, it produced no results and began to be boresome.

It was petty, but I disliked to be beaten, because of my dislike for Quigley. I obtained the prunes by a method which was neither sportsmanlike nor amusing.

I represented the matter unfairly to responsible friends outside, implying that I was being persecuted. They wrote formally to the president of the institution, and shortly afterward prunes were put on my menu.

"You know, of course, that you've made an enemy of Quigley," a friend on the staff told me soon afterward. It seemed that the letter had come up at a staff meeting. The president had been impatient. He had said it was too silly to have been made an issue, and had added, among other things, that prunes were the cheapest articles on the food list.

Some weeks later Dr. Quigley considerably distressed my New York friends by reporting in response to an inquiry concerning my progress:

"Well, he *seems* to be making progress, but we are afraid there is a problem much more serious than drink. He has fixations, obsessions, and if he is crossed about the most trivial matter, he turns vicious, threatens to become violent. He threatened to set the place afire, which is, as you know, an indicative symptom. And if, on the contrary, he is humored, he gloats with a sadistic glee."

This prune episode is a bit silly, but it led to later consequences between Quigley and me. He tried to make me pay for it, but our antipathy and unfairness were mutual. I made him pay for it too, all I could. I still take pleasure in being unfair to him. I'll be as unfair as I possibly can, without telling actual lies, when I recount our subsequent squabbles.

VI

OUR COLLEGE was co-educational, so to speak, but the wings were so widely separated and the grounds so hundred-acre spacious that we seldom came in contact with the Ophelias, except at church and dances. And since church was optional in our queer world, while dances were compulsory, it was at a Saturday evening dance in the chapel-auditorium that I first mingled—as much as the watchful attendants would let me—with the lady patients.

As "Doctor" Diesel had said in the prolonged bath, there were certainly some high-stepping good-lookers among them. The festivities were well under way when our Hall Four delegation entered, shepherded by Miss Pine and Mr. Dirk. To my uninitiate eye, it resembled any not-too-formal dance at a big hotel or country club—except that nobody was soused. There was an excellent jazz orchestra with saxophones and crooners, the floor was crowded with gay couples, kaleidoscopic semi-evening gowns with here and there a stunning décolleté ballroom costume, the usual sprinkling of dinner coats, the usual gayety and chatter. There wasn't a nurse in uniform or white-jacketed attendant anywhere in sight. Miss Pine wore slinky black with spangles and Mr. Dirk looked like a Chautauqua lecturer in a coat with tails.

But all this normal similarity to casual dances in the great wide world outside was superficial as I soon found out, under the tutelage of the disguised superintendent and Miss Pine, who kept a close eye on me, and made me gradually aware that the rules of etiquette were bewilderingly complicated along lines which bore no relation to Confucius or Emily Post.

I noticed an unusualness in the disposal of the crowd as soon as an intermission came in the dancing. Some few couples still strolled, but generally the women were grouped or seated together on the far side of the dance floor while the men remained like a Rotary club convention on our own side. Someone came along and gave me a little dance card with a tiny pencil, and I noticed that everybody had them.

Mr. Dirk said:

"Would you care to dance? I'll introduce you to some of the ladies."

I said:

"Yes—with that red-haired one over there, in the green dress."

"Which one?"

I pointed, but I didn't see much need to point. She registered. She was a tall, curved strawberry blonde with a skin like peaches and cream, big, green panther's eyes which matched her dress, and hair like a maple tree in flame.

Dirk said:

"I want to introduce you first to Miss Simpkins, here. She's one of our best dancers."

Miss Simpkins was a nice homely nurse who didn't seem to care whether I danced with her or not, and I refused to be side-tracked. I told him I wanted to meet the one in green. I told him I thought I had met her before, in Paris. Anyway, I wanted to meet her now and dance with her. Dirk called Miss Pine and tried to side-track me again, and when I wouldn't be side-tracked, he whispered:

"I'm sorry, but, you see, she's a patient."

"Well, my God," I said, "what did you think I thought she was? I'm a patient too. I want to dance with her."

"You don't understand," said Dirk, "patients do not dance with patients."

"What?" I said. "Well, who was she dancing with just now? Wasn't that a patient?"

"Why, no, that was Mr. Harrigan, one of the attendants on Hall Seven. You see, the women patients dance with the male nurses, the male attendants, the staff, the doctors sometimes; and the men patients dance with the female nurses, the dietitians, the female staff, and with the doctors' wives who sometimes come to the dances too."

I said, applying this:

"You mean that you or Gilmore, or any of your damned gorillas, or that prize-fighter, Dan, who sticks me under the nozzle in hydrotherapy can dance with her and that I can't?"

"What's the matter with you?" said Mr. Dirk. "What do you mean, 'her'? I was trying to tell you the general rules."

"Well, how in hell can anybody apply the rules when you all come here disguised? How could I tell you from a case on Hall Eight or Miss Pine there from a part of the Mad Scene in *Lucia* unless I already knew your faces? Most of the mob here have strange faces, and they all look alike to me, or more so."

"Well, don't lie awake about that," said Dirk. "We'll take care of it. Say, why don't you just dance with Miss Pine and shut up for a while? You'd have to look a long way around here, or outside either, to find . . ."

"Say, for cripe's sake," I said, "I was in the war. Dancing with beautiful nurses is no treat to me. I didn't drink myself into a nut college to dance with nurses."

The music began again and they left me. When the floor began to fill, I edged around to where the green dress was sitting, and said:

"May I have this dance?"

She was lovely. As we danced, she said:

"Are you a new doctor?"

I had no chance to answer her. We had only danced about ten steps when Miss Pine and a disguised male attendant blocked us. There was no disturbance, but before I knew what had happened, my beautiful partner had glided away with the attendant and Miss Pine was saying out of the corner of her mouth:

"Come on, you bum. Paschall wants to see you."

He had been dancing with a very attractive patient himself. Dirk had reported our conversation to him—though I didn't know that part of it—and he was sore.

So I said:

"I'm awfully sorry. It was a mistake. I thought she

was one of the dietitians. She looked good enough to eat."

He said:

"Look here, fellow, you've got to cut this out. We won't stand for it. . . . I won't stand for it . . . a minute. You'll get yourself in trouble . . . and me . . . and you won't like it."

"I'm really sorry," I said. "Please forget it. You can forget it. Dirk told me the rules."

"I know what Dirk told you . . . and what you told him. That's why I'm sore. And, believe me, you're going to cut it. If you want to dance with wild women, you'll have to wait until you get back with your own crowd outside."

"Well, do I have to dance with the nurses?"

"No, you don't have to dance at all. If you want to sit like a stick that's your own business. But you have to sit politely. You can't bring a book and read or do crossword puzzles. But what's the matter with the nurses? Only yesterday you were raving about Sally Pine and there are plenty of others here who . . ."

"I'm sorry," I said. "There's nothing the matter with them. It's my own fault that they're policemen to me. But I don't enjoy dancing with cops. With your permission, I'll sit and watch awhile."

I went back to the sidelines and found a chair beside Spike and began to study the spectacle. The orchestra was in full swing again and the floor was crowded.

"Every time you see a man and woman dancing together," said Spike, "one is a patient and the other is an attendant, or a member of the staff, male or female. But not quite always. The doctors sometimes dance with their own wives, or with each other's wives, and the doctors' wives sometimes dance with patients too. Then you may see two nurses, male and female, dance in together to break up something out on the floor, as they did with you just now—sure, I saw it—things like that are happening all the time, but the policing works so smoothly that you seldom notice anything unless you are watching for it. Generally speaking, though, when you see a couple dancing, you can figure that the lady is a nut and the gentleman a cop, or vice versa. Of course, you'll end by getting to know who everybody is, by sight at least, and then it will be simple."

Meanwhile I watched, and knowing very few of the faces it became a bewildering guessing game in which phrenology, physiology, clothing, behavior should have furnished clues, but apparently only made it harder.

Out of my first ten guesses, which Spike checked on, I was wrong seven times. Miss Pine came and sat with us, and we told her the game and the score. Another fox trot began and I tried to improve my average. There were several I was sure I couldn't be wrong on —a microcephalic, giggling hatchet-faced blonde with her hair bobbed like Joan of Arc, an open-mouthed young man with adenoids and steel-rimmed spectacles who looked like the village idiot after he had set fire to the barn in a way-down-east melodrama, and an elated, screen-conscious young creature with Diesel engine eyes who labored under the hallucination that she was Greta Garbo.

I indicated them discreetly to Miss Pine, and said that at any rate anybody could recognize them as patients.

"Yeah," she said, "well, you'd better not let them hear you say so. The first is a graduate nurse from Bellevue, the man is a student nurse planning to be a psychiatrist, and your Garbo is a superintendent in the diet kitchen."

I was discouraged. Instead of venturing any more guesses, I began humbly asking Spike or Miss Pine who various people were, and which side of the fence they were on. It was even more discouraging. It would have been more discouraging to Lombroso, I think, than it was to me. A strikingly handsome gentleman with wide-set, intelligent, kindly eyes and a splendidly shaped head who might have been the director of as big an institution as this one, proved to be a doctor all right, with a long record of achievements listed after his name in *Who's Who*. Spike told me—only he was a schizophrenic. He had spells. He was on Hall Eight. And the most magnificently shaped male head in the whole ballroom was that of the old major. He was a West Pointer from the South who had handled field artillery in the Spanish-American War, in the Philippines and on the Western front in France. Now he played with paper dolls and sometimes thought he was a little girl in pinafores. He enjoyed the Virginia reels, but was inclined to ask gentlemen to waltz with him.

Continuing to watch the dance, I found that while guessing was no good, I had a key that would eventually solve all the puzzles, place all the dancers in their proper categories. I knew already a score or more of individuals among both staff and patients, and each time I saw one of these individuals, Miss Pine, Dirk, or fellow patients from my own hall, for instance, dancing with a new partner, I could classify the part-

ner. Guessing was absolutely useless. I became convinced, and still am, that functional mental derangement, generally speaking, has no physiological, facial
or cranial stigma. Congenital idiots, hydrocephalics,
born imbeciles, of course have. But we had none such
in our asylum. We were all cases who had gone off our
trolleys, as it were, or had broken an axle, or had a
monkey-wrench thrown in our gears, or had lost control, or had gone haywire, not been *born* so. And I as-
sure you that we were indistinguishable to the naked
eye from our keepers and attendants or from any average crowd on the outside, except when one, or a group
of us, started to do our special stuff. And at these
dances, we were generally on our good behavior. We
enjoyed them. At quarter to ten, they gave us ice
cream and cake, and let us stay up if we were good
until nearly ten-thirty instead of being put to bed at
nine.

We were very good at the first dance I attended.
There was less rough-house and disorder than at most
night clubs. Occasionally patients insisted on dancing
with each other and had to be quietly separated; once
or twice couples of young female patients, girl dancing
with girl, lent a Sapphic tinge of violet to the kaleidoscopic scene until they were politely broken by male

attendants who continued the dance with them, and once a young society miss, whose mamma had sent her here to discourage the habit, tried pulling her skirts above her waist, but these contretemps were so smoothly handled that they scarcely caused a ripple, so that bouncers, policemen and the fire department were neither in evidence nor needed.

It was all so restrainedly gay, friendly, normal and pleasant that when I got over my first bewilderment about identities—and my first resentment that I couldn't dance with a beautiful red-haired maniac— I could almost forget that it was special. I still think, after attending many of these dances, that they were handled well—that they were something of which the institution could be justly proud, something to which modern institutional psychiatry can point with pride. Had you been a privileged visitor—such as we rarely had—and looked in at the door for a quarter of an hour, or strolled through with our director, I think you would have marveled that there was so little to marvel at.

Toward the end of the dance, I noticed a lovely girl of unmistakable breeding, background, poise, who was surely a patient since I had seen her dancing with members of the staff, and who was now chatting with some of the head doctors who beamed on her with what seemed to be a pleased mixture of deference and pride. I saw Miss Pine staring at her too, and asked who she was.

Miss Pine said:

"Eight months ago, when I was working on the women's side, it took four of us to put her in a pack. She used to scream all night. She's going out cured next week, completely cured. You'll see her picture before long in the society columns of the New York papers, saying she has come back from Europe. She is supposed to have been in Switzerland. She's married. Her husband comes out every week with her own mother. They come in a Rolls-Royce with a uniformed chauffeur, an old man, with a gray mustache, who doesn't look as if he'll ever tell it."

I haven't told it either. I have told it with absolute essential truth, but the city was not New York and the country was not Switzerland and the Rolls-Royce was an Isotta-Fraschini.

VII

HAVING first seen our auditorium-chapel as a Saturday night ballroom, curiosity soon led me back to see it as a church on Sunday. I need never have gone. It was the one and only thing about which we were absolutely free to do as we pleased. They dragged us to dances and movies, made us go to concerts and forced us to play ping-pong, squash and indoor tennis as ruthlessly as they made us take our medicine and eat our spinach, but whether we went to church or not was a matter of candid and complete indifference to our doctors and attendants alike.

Divine service was held every Sunday afternoon from two-thirty to three-thirty—it had to be in the afternoon because they hired a regular preacher and small choir from outside—and we mostly attended to look at the women patients, as the women patients attended to look at us.

The first day I went along, Miss Pine piloted our

Hall Four delegation, through the long bare corridor leading to the barber-shop, then up a flight of stairs, then onward through the length of Hall Two which was the de luxe Hall inhabited by patients who were so improved that in a few months . . . or a few weeks . . . more they might be discharged as cured. Its windows were not barred; it had a billiard room, card room, radio, library; its bedrooms, with doors opening wide on the long lobby, had writing tables, armchairs, reading lamps, and its patients, though still under restraint, seemed to enjoy a club-like liberty.

I'd probably be transferred there in a couple of months.

Passing on through another bare, connecting corridor, we reached the chapel. Pews were ranged solidly on the erstwhile dance floor, the curtained stage was a pulpit, and in the rear was an organ loft with a little pipe-organ playing a soothing innocuous prelude.

The pews were already two-thirds filled, and I noticed that the males were as sharply divided from the females as in the West Virginian country Dunkard churches I had seen in childhood. These Dunkard churches used to have a "snorting pole" which ran the length of the wide central aisle, with the men all on one side and the women on the other. Families separated at the entrance, wife and daughters joined the other wives and daughters, while husbands and sons, even tots, shunted to the male side with their fellow-farmers. Here we had no actual railing down the central aisle, but the women came in from the opposite side and stayed on the opposite side, while we stayed on ours.

The women patients, I noticed, were all in street clothes, some fashionable and elegant, some dowdy, hats, gloves, hand-bags with powder compacts and mirrors which they used to inspect themselves, and us, without too much craning, though heads turned continually, whispering and smiling. Patients had their romantic "crushes" on other patients, more frequently on nurses or attendants. On the back rows were some old Hogarth ladies, and one who made motions of paring her nails *à la* Rembrandt. The doctors seldom came to church, and I soon discovered why.

The clergyman appeared on the platform, robed, Episcopalian, and began the ritual which was modified High Church, mild and deleted, a formalized and pleasing form of dignified worship which could scarcely displease or excite anybody. Individual patients occasionally had to be "shushed" for responding too loudly or interrupting the preacher. Nurses and male attendants, uniformed and white-coated, were scattered among us to keep us in order. We were restive, but no more so than children. Miss Pine had to take a big black cigar away from Mr. Biemann who chewed it and kept asking out loud for matches, and occasional patients groaned, muttered or suffered in undertones, but not much, and the little was drowned in the droning responses and music.

It was when silence settled upon us presently and the Reverend Percival Bone began his little sermon that I understood why the doctors never came to church. I listened in growing amazement. It was a discourse in monotones from which all religious fervor, all mystical element, all soul, all heaven and all hell, all God and Devil, all reference to Good and Evil—all sequential thought or idea of any sort—were as completely absent as in the babbling of a brook or the whispering of wind in trees. Sometimes, by following his words closely, it would seem that they might be on the verge of meaning something, as when he said, "Hope makes you cheerful so that when you hope you are cheerful, and when you are cheerful you hope, so let us be of good hope and cheerful," but the voice droned on, soothingly, elusively, non sequitur, to love and charity, and I noticed that Miss Pine, breathing softly, was asleep.

I was so puzzled by the Reverend Percival Bone

that I went back to hear him many times. It was always the same. I formed theories. It was impossible, of course, that any man had been able to graduate, even from a theological seminary, with a mind as completely a blank as his seemed to be. It was impossible, for that matter, that he could have put on his shoes in the morning and found his way unguided to a given place. Yet he held a regular job in some regular church outside. I wondered if he took drugs. I wondered if he thought all patients in such institutions lived in a complete mental vacuum and was putting something over on the board of directors since none of the doctors came to check up on him. I wondered if he were himself an automaton, a life inmate himself on one of the back halls, and whether it was the directors who were putting something over on us to save hiring a regular preacher. Even that wild idea seemed possible, for he went through the whole service like a robot or a waxworks image with a phonograph concealed in its chest.

I eventually discovered, or rather learned, that it was all as deliberate and intentional as *Four Saints in Three Acts* or "a rose is a rose is a rose." The Reverend Percival Bone was an intelligent and worthy clergyman, carefully chosen by the board and paid an excellent honorarium to follow their specific, scientific, ultra-modern psychological instructions. Our advanced psychiatrists, some of them ranking among the best in the world and wise in institutional experience, were agreed that religious excitement, religious stimulation, religious fervor or anything which might arouse a fervent, lively interest in religious matters of any sort, was generally very bad medicine for mentally deranged people. Their job, they conceived, was our salvation in this world, restoring us sound to our families. Their minds were single-tracked on that problem. And our heavenly welfare could wait. But they were not atheistic or inimical to religion per se, nor would it have been seemly to deny all patients, though prisoners, the right to attend Christian service in a Christian country. Hence the innocuous compromise.

A somewhat similar policy prevailed concerning the movies which were provided for us, in the same auditorium, fortnightly through the winter. The censorship had no moral, ethical uplift or educational angle. The object was simply to provide us with gentle entertainment, never too exciting. If Mae West and *The Thin Man* were banned, so were *Joan of Arc* and *Ben Hur*. The choice of films lay with a woman doctor of the staff who seemed to have a theory that photoplays starring domestic animals were particularly

soothing to the insane, so over and over again, the hero
was a horse, when it wasn't Rin-Tin-Tin or a Terhune
collie. Lions and tigers at liberty never, but she often
included Mickey Mouse in the programs, to our delight, since mice in a sense live in houses, and once she
gave us a Walt Disney version of Noah's Ark with
lions, tigers, hippos and a polecat, being two-dimen-
sional cardboard lions temporarily domestic for the
period of the voyage.

It was in December, if I mistake not, that she presented Katharine Hepburn in *Little Women*, and
thereby caused a riot. We thought we knew why she
showed us Katharine Hepburn, but it was the picture
itself, not the why of it, that caused the disorder. We
figured it out this way on Hall Four: *The New
Yorker*, which came regularly to the reading room,
had a cartoon showing a bay filly with bangs which
gave itself airs and snooted the rest of the colts in the
paddock because somebody had told her she looked
like Katharine Hepburn. The cartoonist had managed
to give the filly a striking resemblance to Miss Hepburn, or, if you care to twist it around, had succeeded
in making Miss Hepburn look like a horse, and when
Little Women was announced for the following
Thursday, Spike convinced us that it was not a coinci-
dence.

The riot occurred at the point in the picture where the little women gave away their breakfast. If you recall it, the dear little girls had been up since dawn helping mamma, and had just sat down to a pretty breakfast table with steaming coffee, waffles, honey and other delightful breakfast dishes, when Miss Hepburn, whose bangs and cheek-bones did make her look like a pony, conceived the bright idea of giving the whole breakfast, coffee pot and all, to a poorer family next door. As the younger sisters danced around with delight, denuding the table, a girl over in the darkness among the women patients cried:

"Why, it's disgusting! *I'd* have one cup of coffee first, or I'd pour the whole pot down her neck! The idea!"

Spike who was sitting near me, shouted back:

"You said it, sister!"

And the dear old major from Virginia roared distinctly before the hubbub became general and the lights went up:

"If I had a bunch of daughters like that, I'd put 'em in a cat-house!"

"For shame!" cried an old lady patient. "It was beautiful. It was unselfish! It was . . ."

"It was too damned unselfish," somebody else shouted, and then in less loud voices we all began a free-for-all debate, in which the general consensus of opinion seemed to be that it was too much. Luncheon? Sure! Dinner, maybe. But breakfast? It wasn't human. We felt we had been outraged, and continued the argument until we were packed off to bed. Papa Renwick had a headache next day and complained that he hadn't been able to close his eyes all night.

Thereafter our heroes and heroines were quadrupeds, who were sometimes beautifully unselfish too, and sometimes gave away their lives, but never their morning oats.

Occasionally we had concerts provided through Chautauqua or lyceum bureaus. These also seemed— to me at least—a part of the curious, almost Peter-Ibbetsonian return-to-childhood atmosphere of the institution. They took me back to long-forgotten small-town memories of Newberry, South Carolina; Winchester, Virginia; Abilene, Kansas, in the nineties. There was a trio, for instance, of sad, pathetic, smiling women instrumentalists, who tried to be young and pleasing with marcelled hair, who played *Listen to the Mocking Bird*, Chaminade and selections from *Il Trovatore* on harp, violin and flute. They did not

play badly. It was melodic and nostalgic. It seemed to
be the same trio I had been taken by my mother to
hear and see under Alkahest Lyceum auspices in the
Newberry opera house before the Spanish-American
War. They had been young-old women then. Forty
years had passed and they seemed to be the same
young-old women now. They hadn't grown entirely
old and died. Perhaps they couldn't afford to. They
and all their like had disappeared completely from my
ken when I had ceased to be a child in small towns,
and I was unaware that such troubadors still existed.
This was what had become of them. They played now
for institutions of this sort. So, also, on another evening sang a quartet of young-old gentlemen in shabby-
genteel "dress suits" who lifted their eyebrows, and
locked arms, and were good-fellows when they interspersed "classic" songs with mildly humorous numbers
in which the bass and tenor were gay and teased each
other and hummed like bees while the baritone told
of a little Chinese boy named Ah Sing who mistook a
bumblebee for a new kind of butterfly. They were a
dream too, out of my childhood, like the decayed,
plump woman playing Chaminade on a harp. I saw
them less naïvely now. It was painful when they
bowed to the applause and made their worn faces

smile, turning the smiles on and off as if pressing a
mechanical device. I wonder what they thought about
us. I wonder whether they pitied us as I pitied them,
or whether they envied us our security when they went
back through the snow to their own world of day
coaches, one-night stands and shabby boarding houses.

Our big park was snow-covered and beautiful now,
and pretty soon with the sunlight gleaming on the
dazzling white hillsides dotted with spruce and fir-
trees outside the steel scrolled bars of our windows, it
was the bright morning of Christmas Eve on Hall
Four. We were busy and happy immediately after
breakfast, for instead of being sent to the workshops,
we were permitted to help with the preparations for
Christmas. A big Christmas tree had been dragged in
and was being set up by Mr. Dirk with the help of a
couple of porters who had also resurrected from the
basement store-rooms a number of boxes packed with
stars, bulbs, tinsel, little angels, papier-mâché drome-
daries, cotton sheep, birds and beasts from Bethlehem
—treasures which most of us had seldom seen and certainly never handled since far-off nursery days—and
Mr. Dirk was encouraging us to help him. Crates of
holly, wreaths, garlands, red ribbon had been carted in
too and we were making the whole place festive. The

professor of histology had at first been inclined to toss the silver-gilded balls to the ceiling, for experimental purposes he said, but had been easily persuaded to desist, and Miss Pine had succeeded with more difficulty in comforting the little lawyer who had sat in a corner weeping rather histrionically because he had murdered Santa Claus. But these incidents were no more than might have happened in any well-regulated nursery, and a little before lunch time, since there were so many of us to help and enjoy doing it, the decoration was nearly all completed. The big tree, now laden with all its bright trinkets, stood almost filling the reading room alcove, and was to be wired later by Mr. Gilmore with little electrical candles.

After luncheon when we were being checked off for a walk in the sunshine with Miss Pine, there were only thirteen of us instead of fourteen, and we discovered that Mr. Biemann was missing. Mr. Biemann was a big, blowsy, popular, blond, middle-aged Teutonic gentleman engaged, I believe, in contracting, until worry over the depression had brought him just a week or so before to our kindergarten. He was always in a bit of a fog, but always sweet and smiling, gentle and lumbering like a sick Saint Bernard. He followed Spike around one day, insisting on tying one of Spike's shoelaces for him, which bothered Spike considerably because he was wearing bedroom slippers which didn't have any shoelaces. And when his family brought him candy, of which he was very fond, he always insisted on finishing the box instantly by the double process of making us all help him eat it on the spot. It made him sick one day and afterward, because we all liked him so much, we connived with the attendants to steal the box away from him, passing him back an empty box or a box that contained only one or two pieces after it had gone one round, and doling it out to him on successive days. He was a queer and lovable German combination of greediness and generosity. He seemed to love us all, both patients and attendants, and had been very happy about its being Christmas. Now he was missing. That is, Dirk had looked in his room, under his bed, in both lavatories and behind the piano. We were all helping hunt for him, and we might have hunted longer if he hadn't characteristically revealed himself. He had hidden in the alcove behind the Christmas tree. He had a handful of silver cherries and gilded bulbs which he was munching, and offered to share them. He had been eating the ornaments off the Christmas tree. His moon-face was smiling and there was a faint, crisp grape-nutsy crackle as his jaws worked.

"My God," said Dirk to Miss Pine, grabbing Mr. Biemann's wrist, "those things are glass, aren't they?"

"No, I don't think so," said Miss Pine, "but we'd better find out. They crack to pieces like glass, but I don't think they cut. They break all up, powdery."

Gilmore meanwhile was phoning, and in two seconds the dot-and-dash electrical code boxes throughout the whole institution, controlled from the office of the telephone operator, were clicking an S O S on behalf of Hall Four. Staff doctors soon began arriving on the run. It was hectic for a moment, because it turned out that none of them knew either, for certain, whether the things were glass or not. They looked inside Mr. Biemann's mouth and found that it was not cut, they crushed two or three of the fragile silver globes in their hands and found that their hands weren't cut either. Relieved, but still uncertain, not knowing what else Mr. Biemann might have eaten off the Christmas tree, they hurried him off to the X-ray room while the rest of us were told everything was all right and sent to walk with Miss Pine. Miss Pine and Spike presently asked what I thought, and I told them I wasn't worrying much because I had once seen Harry Kemp chew up and swallow a teacup in a fit of temper at a party. It turned out that way. Mr. Biemann didn't even have indigestion.

Thus having passed our morning of Christmas Eve trimming the tree and hanging festive garlands, we had our institutional celebration that same evening, so that on Christmas Day itself we would be "free" to have our divers private individual huddles with such members of our family or other personal friends from the outside as might come to visit us.

Before supper, Dirk saw to it that we all put on our best bibs and tuckers, slicked our hair, prettied ourselves up to do him and the occasion credit. The supper likewise was prettied. We had roses and candles, oyster cocktails followed by a pleasant, innocuous pink variation of welsh rabbit which Spike nicknamed "blushing bunny" and of which most of us had two helpings. The fruit salad was festive with maraschino cherries, and the cake served with the sherbet had frosting of two colors. Also we were permitted to light cigarettes at the table, which was generally strictly *verboten*. We were never under any circumstances permitted to possess matches. Miss Pine and Gilmore supplied the fire with Ritz hotel headwaiter mimicry, and we were all millionaires for the moment.

"By ding!" said little Hauser, inhaling, "we've got a booby-hatch de luxe, no kidding!"

And, "Say, fellow," drawled Dirk, "we're glad you

like it, but don't pull stuff like that this evening. The idea is to make you forget it. You know how the doctors feel."

"But that's hooey," said Hauser cheerfully. "I like it fine here, and it's a sign I'm getting well when I know just where I am and can laugh about it."

"Yeah, but . . ." retorted Dirk, and then discreetly pointed. Mr. Benton, one of the older patients at another table, was sitting quietly with his bowed head jerking ever so slightly and tears streaming silently down his cheeks.

"I'm sorry," muttered the kid. It had seemed to me also that the pious camouflage was mostly hooey. It was certainly hooey to Spike and Hauser and me, but now here was Mr. Benton, a perhaps nicer man than any of us and who was further toward being cured of what ailed him than we were, crying in his plate on Christmas Eve because Hauser had said out loud that we were inmates of a hatch. Mr. Benton, who was in no fog at all, knew this perfectly well. Yet it had hurt him to hear it said.

We were all sorry for Mr. Benton, and after supper we tried to cheer him up, and he apologized for crying at the table, and said that what had got him was not so much thinking of other Christmas Eves when children and grandchildren had been gathered around him, but that he had said to himself, "Well, I've spent Christmas in a lot of places in my life—one in Havana where it was hot like summer—but never, never, did I think I would spend Christmas as an inmate in a place like this."

"Well, I guess none of us ever did," said the railroad fireman, and added, looking around at the Christmas tree now lighted and the festive decorations everywhere, "but I guess some of us have spent Christmases in worse places."

The Russian Jew remembered that he had spent a Christmas Eve in jail, and Mr. Barnes remembered sitting all night in a cold Wisconsin railway station, waiting for a snow-delayed train. Comparing our Christmas Eve memories, I found that, being a sort of professional traveler, I could beat them all except the Russian. I recalled a Christmas Eve spent aboard a Dutch freighter off Trinidad when we drank Holland gin and ate hard little sausages all night long; another lost on a donkey in the forest of Khabara trying to reach Timbuctoo from the river; one spent in a shelled village behind Verdun; another with a tribe of Arabs. Then it twisted back, on the fireman's lead, to exchanging memories of the worst Christmas Eves we had ever spent, and the worst I could recall was an uneventful one I had worked through on a morning paper in Atlanta.

What I didn't say was, like Mr. Benton, though without his sentimental sadness, that I had never thought I would spend a Christmas Eve locked up behind the bars, in a place like this. I kept feeling that even if nothing special happened, this would certainly be the strangest Christmas I had ever spent.

From far down the other end of our corridor came Dirk and his attendants, turning out all the lights as they came, dimming all the lights too in the reading room except those on the Christmas tree, telling us the carolers were coming.

Soon they came, a rather solemn and beautiful procession, entering our dark, long corridor through the double doors, women like nuns in white pacing slowly two by two, bearing tall lighted candles, singing, followed by darker figures. At the head of the procession marched, minced, or rather danced in solemn, slow, religious measure, my pet abomination, the department store floorwalker, Dr. Quigley, playing rather well on a fiddle as he marched. He was not in costume; that is, he was dressed as we always saw him making his ordinary rounds, even to the gold-rimmed spectacles on his pinched nose, yet he managed grotesquely to resemble the fiddlers who used to adorn Howard

Pile's fairy tales, with pointed medieval cap and boots, followed usually by foxes. It may have been the way he slowly minced and half-stepped to the solemn measure. The nunlike choristers, arriving closer, proved to be nurses in their usual white uniforms, and behind them marched a motley collection of males recruited for their voices from all branches of the hospital,—attendants, kitchen helpers, some of the doctors, Tim Devlin from the gymnasium, some porters, and at the last, majestically bringing up the rear, our pot-bellied, bearded general superintendent, keeping a shrewd eye on everything and booming the deepest bass of all.

The carol they sang as they came down the long corridor toward us was to the tune of *Tannenbaum*, that is, *Maryland, My Maryland*, and as they came, I began to distinguish the words. At first I couldn't be sure, but before they reached us and swung to the right, I had all the words in place, yet even then could scarcely believe my ears. I thought to myself, "Are they crazy, or are we?" I thought, "Gertrude Stein would like this." For here is what they sang, verbatim:

> *Oh, Christmas tree, oh, Christmas tree,*
> *Oh, Christmas tree, oh, Christmas tree!*

Oh, Christmas tree,
Oh, Christmas tree,
Oh, Christmas tree,
Oh, Christmas tree,
Oh, Christmas tree, oh, Christmas tree,
Oh, Christmas tree, oh, Christmas tree.

They sang it fervently, melodiously, solemnly, and rather well. The pretty ones among the marching nurses lifted their eyes as they marched and tried to resemble Saint Cecilia. It was as good as a sermon by our Reverend Percival Bone. It was as soothing and unlikely to excite us as the movies in which the hero was a horse. Pot-Belly boomed bass through his beard, the most solemnly of all, but as he passed Dirk, one of his heavy eyelids drooped in an even more solemn wink.

Were we kidding them, or were they kidding us? That was the recurrent and ever present problem in this great modern psychiatric institution. We never knew, and I am not sure whether they always knew either.

Next day we said Merry Christmas among ourselves, and to the staff of course, admired the tree again, ate turkey and plum pudding, but what keyed Christmas Day, supplied its chief tone, was the inundation of visitors. All of us had at least one visitor. Some of us had several. Most of them were familiar faces who came every Wednesday or Friday—Hauser's father, Frainer's mother, the wives of the histologist and railroad fireman, Mr. Wylie's brother, Mr. Stacy's worried bride. But today there were extra aunts, cousins, married daughters, remoter connections or friends who had come from a long distance, some of them for the first time.

It was always interesting to study visitors who came inside our locked precincts for the first time. They usually regarded their own patient as a normal invalid, as it were, but all the rest of us with dubious misgivings. They wanted to hurry through our corridors, smoking room, public reception hall, to the privacy of their own patient's bedroom, where they were forced to leave the door open, but conversed in low tones. They were invariably initially embarrassed to be visiting this sort of place, to have one of their "dear ones" shut up in it. They all had the same psychology —the first time. When my friend had come for the first time, she had been most unhappy, terrified, I suspect, that I should be shut up in such a place . . . and unhappier still when I had made the mistake of trying to put her at her ease, to make her feel "at home" there, by taking her into the smoking room, introducing Spike and others of my new playmates, trying to make her feel that I was already "at home" and all right. Instead of being re-assured, she had gone to Paschall afterward in tears:

"It was a terrible mistake to put him in a place like this! Can't you see? He is beginning to be just like the others! He is beginning to look and talk as they do. He is beginning *to be one of them.*"

Before she had come many times, she was bringing Spike cigarettes, laughing at Hauser's comedy, finding that she and the histologist had mutual friends in Paris, listening absorbed when the railroad fireman told of his adventures.

These reversals of attitude on the part of our visitors—initial terror and subsequent reassurance—were sometimes even more striking than in the case of my Marjorie. I recall one case that was like a little Ibsen drama:

When I had been on Four some weeks, a new patient by the name of Kingston had arrived. He was a pleasant little man with sandy hair, about forty-five years old, had a dryly humorous mouth with a kindly twist to it. What might be the matter with him was a mystery—I mean, to us other patients—for he seemed perfectly normal, completely coördinated. I enjoyed talking with him and thus discovered that, somehow, when he was talking most interestingly, it would occur that suddenly a whole flood of words other than those he was using (and with an entirely different context) would come out unconsciously. Then he would become conscious of what was occurring and would attempt to choke them back, until they became frantic, stammering sounds, then ceased, and permitted lucid continuation of what he had consciously been saying.

In a couple of days, his wife came to see him—her first visit. We knew it was his wife because she and Dirk came into the smoking room and got him. She was a bride-like sort of creature, tall, considerably younger, with a sensuously kindly mouth, and big cow-like eyes which somewhat belied the urban sophistication of her smart, tailored clothes.

As Kingston was new, he was still quartered in the wide-open bedroom midway the corridor, immediately opposite Dirk's office, where I had spent a first annoyed public night. Having occasion presently to go to the other end of the corridor, passing this open door, I glanced in without curiosity, and although I turned my eyes away almost instantaneously, beheld a sight not easy to forget. Once, flashing an electric torch in a deep jungle forest, it had revealed two frightened gibbons, clinging to one another, eyes wide, shadowingly dark, mirroring dumb terror of the unknown. So these two humans now were clinging, and the same thing was in their eyes—the look of repressed, would-be mouthwailing fear that superstitious children have—silent, anticipating the hideous and nameless. They were perched on the edge of the bed, and looked indescribably lost, though in so small a room. She had her arm protectively over his shoulders and was holding both his hands. Their eyes were turned toward the door, as if the dreadful thing would enter by it. I doubt that they saw me as I passed. I averted my head automatically. I would bet that the girl's mother, or some of her family, had sympathized with her about the "awful shame" and burden of it, had probably suggested that she had rather see John "in his grave."

It turned out that Kingston's malady, his quirk, his cross-circuiting of cerebral-lingual wires, was no worse a problem to the psychiatrists than a case of double vision would have been for the oculists. Learning this took all the fear out of both of them, and with it the embarrassment and shame. Curing him was going to take a year or so, but by February his wife was coming Wednesdays and Fridays, as cheerful and familiar as you please, helloing the rest of us, asking about our progress, and talking of John's case as freely as if he'd been having a broken elbow straightened or his ribs mended.

Marjorie tells me she went through the same stages, less dramatically. I imagine most visitors, i.e., wives, mothers, fathers, friends, did. In the end, visitors made friends among themselves and fraternized; on the suburban trains coming out, sharing taxis from the village station up to our hill, telling the conductor, the newsstand man, the Greek at the fruit store all about it, when they asked, "How's your patient?"

The town was proud of the place and friendly toward it. It brought the town's only fame, and a lot of business. Marjorie tells me that one day when she was in the doldrums, her taxi driver said:

"Don't you worry, lady; I've seen 'em taken up there in a net or on a stretcher, and I've seen 'em come out in a year or so driving their own cars to start on a new honeymoon."

She says that eventually she didn't give a damn about the sort of place it was, and I noticed that she had dropped using the camouflaged private-box address when she wrote to me. Even the things she ordered sent from Spalding when spring came, or from Brooks Brothers, arrived addressed to me in the place I was in, by the place's own name which is still "Asylum" on the maps if not on their own letterheads.

So that when our crowds of visitors came on Christmas Day, to stay most of the afternoon, we swapped candy, visited among each other, drifted in and out of the smoking room, compared our gifts, and only went into huddles when we had actually private matters to talk about.

The strangest thing to me was to be cold sober on so habitually bibulous a holiday. I'd been getting more or less tight over Christmas as most of my friends did —and I hope still do—for many a long year, before I ever dreamed that I'd later become one of the weak ones who couldn't take it.

God forbid that any of this record be or become a temperance lecture. I still think whiskey is a grand thing. I still believe that no man has ever become a victim of whiskey—but only of some weakness within himself.

VIII

Early in February, they decided that the initial stages of my cure had progressed sufficiently to shift me along to Hall Two where the patients have greater liberty and responsibility. I went reluctantly. I was sure I wouldn't like it, and for some weeks I sulked.

Hall Two was less of a prison, but it was also less of a kindergarten. I missed both atmospheres, the bars and the soft, easy coddling. It was up on a second floor, and while we were all locked in as scrupulously as below, the windows were not steel barred. They merely had screens. We were supposed to have passed the point where we might break windows or smash furniture. We were no longer continually watched. The tempo was entirely different. We no longer had female nurses, were no longer pampered as interesting invalids. The atmosphere was a queer combination of fraternity house and military barracks. The superintendent of the Hall was a pompous, heel-clicking,

Canadian ex-top sergeant, who had worked in big hotels after the World War. His name was Duval. His surface qualities were those of a combination maître d'hôtel and policeman. But he was also an old maid. This he-spinster quality revealed itself in two ways which were paradoxical, but which made him, I suppose, a good man for his special job. He cared so much for the carpets, the polished tables, the arrangements of the chairs, the neatness of his domain, and scolded us so pettishly when we moved things about or left them in disorder, that we sometimes complained bitterly that he had the whole thing backward—that the furniture came first with him and that patients were merely incidental. But this was not true. His other, more secret spinster quality, was a sentimental maternal instinct. He was like a setter dog which had adopted a lot of homeless monkeys. He hated us when we engaged in monkey-business, but he thought he was our mother. When any of us got sick or hurt ourselves, he fluttered like an old hen. Yet being a top-sergeant, a policeman, he never coddled us. Although he was only about forty-five, younger than some of the patients, we all called him "Papa" Duval even to his face when we were feeling friendly toward him. When we were exasperated, we called him "her" behind his

back, referred to him as "Mrs. Duval." I went through
the process that most newly transferred patients did,
of loathing him for a few weeks, and eventually becoming very fond of him.

In fact, I loathed everything on this new hall for
the first few weeks. Instead of the lazy, easy, quiet
(except when somebody began weeping, howling like
a wolf, or seeing his dead grandfather) lobby down
on Hall Four where we could loll about in big stuffed
armchairs or sprawl on couches with pretty nurses to
wait on us, we were forced to sit up and wait on ourselves. The smoking room here was a stiff game-room,
with a pool table in the middle, a radio, card tables,
chess and checker tables, no couches, no armchairs or
easy chairs at all, nothing but straight-backed hard
chairs which we believed they had designed to be as
stiff and uncomfortable as possible. Nevertheless, this
was the room in which we congregated. At the other
end of the lobby was a cheerless, formal "library"
which had armchairs and couches—the long corridors
had big couches too—but since we were not allowed
to lie on the couches, and not permitted to smoke in
the "library," both were usually empty as a Victorian
parlor.

In our bedrooms, we had a little more latitude and

considerably more responsibility than on Hall Four. The doors still remained always open, but the blue night lights in the wall were abolished. We had writing tables, stationery, reading lamps, and nearly all our private clothing and belongings were restored to us. We could not have pocket-knives, matches, or razors, but when we entered this hall our wrist-watches, fountain pens, extra belts, books, clothing, knickknacks, were restored to us. We had to keep all our clothes and belongings in order, make out our own laundry lists, keep our bureau drawers and wardrobes neat. Papa Duval was always mooching about, scolding and seeing to it that we did. Instead of enjoying the greater liberty, I resented this too. I had gotten used to having Miss Pine do everything for me just as my mother used to when I was six, including picking up behind me and telling me when to put on a different shirt or another tie.

What I liked least at first on this Hall was my fellow patients. They were too normal. They were nearly well, or getting well. They lived, talked and deported themselves more or less as I imagine they always had on the outside, so that the social atmosphere was radically different from the hall below. Here there was, if not exactly snobbery, the beginning

of selection and the forming of groups, cliques. Down
below, there had been the basic, leveling camaraderie
of common upset or misfortune. We had been like a
heterogeneous group in a bombarded dugout or war
hospital. When men lie in adjacent beds with machine
gun bullets through their gizzards or snootsful of
chlorine gas, they find other things in common than
having been to Harvard or to Philadelphia to hear
Stokowski. Nobody on Hall Four gave a hoot that
Wethered was in the Social Register and Ryder in the
firemen's union. But up here on Two, we were all
aware of such things, not nastily aware of them, but
aware—as people are on the outside.

There were only seventeen patients on Hall Two
when I was transferred there, yet they were split into
groups. There was a group of five or six intellectuals
who played contract together and wanted to listen to
symphonies and chamber music on the radio. There
was a group of business men, two of them Jewish, who
played pool and pinochle and preferred listening to
Eddie Cantor or Ed Wynn. There were three or four
youths whom everybody was kind to but did not include, and two or three oldsters who moped or read.
They were all decent enough to me, and I could have
grouped as I pleased, but not because I was a fellow

unfortunate, a fellow inmate. I could have grouped as I pleased because I had written a couple of books and had a name which appeared occasionally in the newspapers. Well, I didn't like this. I didn't feel that I was a person who had written a couple of books. I felt that I was a patient locked up where I ought to be, except that I ought to still be down on Hall Four, so I sulked and wished I was back downstairs.

In fact, I even tried to get sent back. Most patients, being perhaps more reasonable and less irritable, were delighted to be moved upstairs, recognizing that it was progress, and if they were afterward sent back to Four, they were disconsolate about it. So that one of their ways of preserving discipline on Two was to threaten to send us back. I really wanted to go back, so on the second afternoon, before we were to be taken for our walk, I went into the deserted library and took a cushion off the couch and sprawled down on the thick-carpeted floor behind the couch and went to sleep. Duval found me, and was quite angry, and telephoned the main office and demanded that I be sent back to Four.

They kept me in from the walk and Paschall soon came up.

"Do you really want to go back to Four?"

"Yes, this is lousy."

I told him all my troubles. I told him I hated the radio and loathed pool or watching other people play pool, and hated to smoke sitting up in a straight, hard chair, and that it was like living in a barracks, or living in a Y.M.C.A. or a Phi Gamma Delta frat house with all the comfortable couches removed.

"Sure it's not Sally Pine?" he asked.

"Why, sure it is," I said. "That's part of it. I like to look at her. But I like everybody down there better than up here."

"Wait a minute," he said, "we think we've pampered you about enough. We think you're soft. Did you come here to be cured or to loaf? Do you want to go soft entirely and be a hospital case all your life with nurses looking after you? The chairs up here are hard for a reason. It's time you began to learn to sit up straight again. And it's time for you to begin to be able to hear a radio you don't like and mix with sensible people whether you want to or not. You'll have to do it on the outside, you know, unless you just go out and drink yourself to death. By the way, we're not going to put you back on Four. You're not a mental case. You know what you're doing. But we know what we're doing too. You will either stay on this hall and behave yourself—and obey the rules—or we'll notify your friends on the outside to take you out and put you somewhere else. You're committed, but we don't have to keep incurables. They'll just have to get you locked up somewhere else."

"You win," I said, "but I liked it better on Hall Four."

So I became a routine, polite, if slightly surly patient on Hall Two, but refused to be a member of "Papa" Duval's family, and avoided the recreation room except when I went in to smoke. I still went daily, now with my new group, to the workshops at 8:30 in the morning, thence to the gymnasium and showers before luncheon, and to walk in the early afternoons, but this was in early February, turning dark soon after four o'clock, and from late afternoon until bedtime we were locked in the hall with nothing to do but play billiards, pool, bridge, chess and checkers, read books or magazines, listen to the radio, converse, write letters, or sit and mope as it pleased our fancy. Curfew here was at ten instead of nine o'clock, so that it made a long stretch broken only by supper which still came at 5:30.

I moped, read long, old books like *David Copperfield* and *Clarissa Harlowe* in the empty, cheerless li-

brary; was depressed and knew that if I were outside
or in an ordinary sanitarium where attendants could
be bribed to bring in whiskey, I would soon be drinking like a fish again.

This demeanor, of course, was observed by Duval
and put down on my daily chart, observed likewise by
the doctors on their rounds. Down on Hall Four, after
the first adjustment and long, torturing hangover, I
had been cheerful as a kid who belonged to the gang,
liked everybody and was liked by them, sharing cigarettes, swapping lies, quarreling and kidding, so that
my depression now was all the more noticeable.

Paschall, who was puzzled and annoyed, came one
day and told me that Quigley was going to haul me
before the staff. Quigley felt, he said, that I was being
deliberately troublesome, "not coöperating." He
added, impatiently, that he was inclined to believe
Quigley was right, so that when I was escorted down
to the conference room that afternoon, I anticipated a
sort of general court-martial, a general bawling out.
But it was not like that. It was really a part of the
routine for them. All patients, at times when they
showed sudden marked regression—or sudden marked
improvement either—were brought before the board.
Pot-Belly presided benevolently, and there were a

dozen or so doctors, most of whom I knew by sight, including two psychoanalysts and a woman. They asked amiable questions, but I was embarrassed and stuffy. I don't know that I could have shed much light for them on my own problem, anyway. The questions all led toward three basic things they wanted light on:

Why had I ever become a drunkard?

Why I didn't like it on Hall Two?

And whether I myself felt that I had made some progress toward cure since entering the institution?

It was only the third question that I could answer categorically. I told them that I sincerely believed that, although I had now been in the institution for considerably more than two months, no progress whatever had been made toward my cure. My physical nerves were less jangled, my hands and mouth had stopped trembling, my general physical condition was perhaps improved, but this was merely because I hadn't been drinking anything for two long months, and the *only reason I hadn't been drinking anything was that I had been locked up where I couldn't get it.*

"Well, that's something, isn't it?" asked Pot-Belly.

"I don't know whether it is or not," I said. "I'd just as soon die as to be locked up all my life."

"It takes time," he said, and when it was over,

Paschall, who had merely listened, said, "Well, I certainly wasn't proud of you."

I know a good deal more now than I did then, and I am inclined to believe that perhaps the only thing these doctors or anybody can now do for a certain type of drunkard is precisely to lock him up where he can't get it. The method is beautifully pragmatic. . . . It is 100 per cent efficient. "Papa is killing himself drinking! How can we make him stop?" "The dog runs away. How can we make it stay at home?" Well, there may be many ways, through kindness, love, scolding, various sorts of treatment, moral or immoral suasion, by which you *may* or *might* be able to make the dog stop running away and papa stop drinking himself to death. But chain up the dog, by God, and he *won't* run away. Lock papa up where he can't get a drink, can't bribe, can't break out, can't distill or ferment it himself, and, Q.E.D., papa will stop drinking. He'll stop as long as he's locked up, anyway, and if you keep him locked up long enough, he may get out of the habit. Of course, by the use of such methods, you can similarly make a man stop eating or stop living. You can break him of the habit of eating so that he'll never eat any more. You can break him of the habit of drawing his breath if you lock him in a

vacuum. But desperate cases require desperate reme-
dies. And any man's case is desperate, de facto, when
liquor has really got him down.

I am inclined to believe that no man is a drunkard
until he drinks, hating it, in the mornings. Then he is
an addict in the drug-sense. Of course, "mornings" is
an arbitrary way of putting it. It is merely repeating
that no man is a drunkard until he has to drink when
he doesn't want to. Never take a drink when you *need
it*, and you'll never be a drunkard though you come
home pie-eyed four nights out of seven. It's lots of fun
to get drunk in good company when you enjoy it. I
don't like teetotalers. I am middle-aged. I drank for
twenty years, enjoying it, doing good work and never
getting into trouble. I hope, before I die, to be able to
drink again and enjoy it. If I have been really cured,
I shall. If not, I shall perhaps be a teetotaler as rup-
tured people wear trusses; I shall use teetotalism as a
crutch.

Paschall came up the day after the conference to
see what he could drag out of me in a private conversation. He was friendly, but puzzled, impatient, and
somewhat disgusted.

He invited confidence, and I tried to give it to him.
I said:

"I'm bored. You think I'm bored from being locked up, now that the novelty has worn off. You tell me the trouble with drunks is that they always get bored by the restraint and think they're cured and want to go home when all they've done is get over their headaches. But I don't think I'm cured, and I wasn't ever bored on Four. I liked it. Now I'm bored on this hall. The patients bore me. They talk about Wall Street and Walter Lippmann, or Culbertson or golf. They play contract and billiards and ping-pong. I didn't come here to play contract and talk about the stock market. I used to do things like that when I was a Rotarian in Atlanta. But I don't like them any more. It's like being sick in a club or a frat house."

Paschall lighted a cigarette and said:

"I think I begin to see what it's about, but for a man past forty-five you seem to have the emotional reactions if not the mind of a child. You miss your little playmates. You miss the fun and irresponsibility on Hall Four. You miss the comedy and occasional excitement. It was high time we moved you off that Hall. You need to take us and yourself more seriously. The patients who bore you up here are all right. The trouble's with you. You played contract downstairs where they redouble seven no trumps and lead the queen of hippogriffs, but up here where they play real contract, you refuse to play. And there's big news coming every day from Washington. It wouldn't hurt you to read Walter Lippmann and talk with your fellow patients about the New Deal. Don't sneer. I mean it. It's your country. You may get out of here some day and go back to work.

"By the way," he continued, "your friends Hauser and Spike will be moving up here in a couple of days, and you won't be so lonesome. Johnny Reiss seems better since you left—maybe cause and effect—and it won't be long before he comes along too, but I doubt whether Duval will let you set up another shoeshine parlor."

Paschall, I think, was more or less right. I missed my playmates. This Johnny Reiss was a grand kid, though spectacular. For a while prior to my own commitment, he had been a problem on Hall Eight, which was the wild ward. He was childishly blond, not yet twenty-one, of medium height, compactly built and muscled like a bobcat. His widowed mother ran a workmen's boarding house in Hoboken, and the kid, after starring on all his high school teams, had stayed on as assistant to the physical director, until he missed a flying leap, and landed on his head. No cranial bones were broken, but when he came to, in a hospital, he was crazier than Tarzan of the Apes. They had netted him and brought him here, and he had been a handful, so the backhall attendants told me. They actually bragged about him. He was sweet-natured as a puppy, but believed that he was one of Custer's men fighting redskins, and every little while, mistaking the attendants or his fellow patients for Apaches in warpaint, he would make a "last stand." These transitions occurred suddenly, and since his heroic idea of a "last stand" was kinetic, two fast, wrestling attendants remained always within grabbing distance, to catch him in mid-air. He had Indians "on the brain," and was continually surrounded by them, but a step forward was achieved when the doctors, unable to disperse the Indians, persuaded Johnny they were friendly Indians. So, for a while, instead of making "last stands" he began to study Indian lore with friendly chiefs, practicing war whoops and rain-dances. A little later, they told me—nobody knew exactly why—he had given up Indians. They had all disappeared, and as he was good-natured and happy, they had moved him over to Hall Four. He now believed that he was in a musical conservatory in Pittsburgh and that Miss Pine was his sister. That is, he believed this most of the time. At

intervals, he didn't know where he was, and wondered
what it was all about. He was coördinated physically,
if not yet mentally, went with us on walks and to the
gymnasium, and whichever side he played on in volley ball always won.

The Reiss-Seabrook Shoeshine Parlor, Limited,
about which Paschall twitted me, had been organized
one Sunday morning as the result of an impulse on
Johnny's part. All the credit was his. A fixed tradition
in our institution was that all patients, whether millionaire or charity—and we had both—must keep their
own shoes clean and polished. Regularly on Sunday
mornings, Dirk lugged in two oversize bootblack
boxes, containing all the necessary pastes, brushes,
cloths, etc., and placed them on spread-out newspapers, in the middle of the smoking room. We kidded
each other, made it a diversion. Several of the crowd,
born in New York, confided that they had never
shined their own shoes before, not even when they
were so broke they had to count the nickels. That particular morning, when I happened to be one of the
first, old Mr. Wylie, bending over the adjacent box,
was groaning rheumatically. I noticed that his face
twitched with real pain, and said, "Here, I'll just fin-
ish that for you." He demurred and then let me, with

a sigh of grateful relief. I got down on one knee, when Johnny Reiss came, filled with delight, to supervise it. He didn't like the way I was doing it, toppled me over as if we were a couple of puppies, and did it himself, talking wop, flourishing his elbows, spitting professionally through his teeth—and then insisted on doing mine. I said, "Hell, Johnny, if you do, I'll have to shine yours."

"Sure," he replied, and went to it. The others now gathered round, offering comments, and Johnny said, "Jesus, look at the clients! Let's start a shoeshine parlor." So we did, taking them all in turn. Some of them were embarrassed, ashamed for us and consequently unwilling, but in the end they all let us do it. In the midst of it Dirk, who had been in the kitchen, turned up with a "What's going on here?" and seemed inclined to stop us, but I guess he was unable to think of any rule which applied to a case so unforeseen, and contented himself with writing it down on our charts, and we never heard any more about it.

We had had a good time on Hall Four. Diversions and mild disorders had occurred there continually. Now nothing seemed to happen on Hall Two—until one night, when I'd been there only about a fortnight, plenty happened. It taught me, incidentally, that I had been mistaken again. It reconciled me to my new surroundings—partly because it had "Papa" Duval in a panic.

We all knew something was the matter during supper, but we didn't know what. All we knew was that Duval was scared, nervous and angry, that Fagan, the chief of the gorillas, had been up on the hall, that Pot-Belly had come, and that there had been muffle-voiced telephoning. We counted noses in the dining room, and we were all there. Nobody knew anything. Not even Spike, who had meanwhile been transferred up from Four as promised.

After supper, we all went to the smoking room, but Spike happened to go down to the usually lighted but abandoned library at the far end of the corridor to fetch a magazine. He came back loudly telling the world that the library was dark with its big double doors closed and locked. He wanted to know why. We all wanted to know why. We all suddenly demanded books or magazines.

The night force came on ahead of time, but Duval didn't leave. Maybe an attendant leaked, or maybe not. We were all in the smoking room, every one of

us, buzzing, whispering, and pretty soon, by clairvoy-
ance, grapevine telegraph—probably an attendant
merely leaked—we all knew everything, or thought
we did. Somebody had tried to escape by way of the
library. I have explained, I believe, that our hall was
on a high second floor, forty feet above the ground,
and that the windows were solidly screened, but
not barred. Well, somebody had cut or filed a screen
in one of the library windows, and knotted sheets
(filched from the outgoing wash which was sometimes
stacked outside the linen room) had been found hidden behind the library divan. This, by the way, though
we had it as yet only as tenuous guess-gossiping, was
more or less exactly what had happened. And what
made it the more interesting, as we counted each
other's noses again in the smoking room, was that one
of us, still there present, had done it, had planned the
escape for that same night. We looked at each other
and guessed our best, drifted into huddles comparing
guesses, until Spike presently began guessing out loud.
"There's any one of five of us who might have done
it," he said, "but only five out of the seventeen of us,"
he added with conviction.

"Yeah, well, are you one of the five?" asked one of
the Culbertson experts.

"Yes, I am," said Spike. "It happens I didn't do it, but I'm the only one who knows that, and you needn't believe me, so I should be counted as one of the five. Sure, I'll name the other four, and bet you a pack of cigarettes it lays among the five of us."

He named names, including mine, as the last of the list, but including it. I wanted to know why, and he said:

"I don't think you did it, but you are a suspect, you'll see. The doctors are working on all our charts right now. They'll be along in a minute, and you'll see. Number 1, you hate this hall, you hate Duval, and you've said so. Number 2, you're a drunk, and all drunks get fed up and want to get out as soon as they've been here long enough to get sober. Number 3, you're a professional adventurer."

All the other patients were eyeing me, speculatively, with interest, but without affection.

I said:

"Well, by God, Spike, it sounds plausible. Maybe I did do it."

"No, you didn't," said Spike, "but you're a legitimate suspect." Just then Pot-Belly marched by the door, accompanied by Drs. Quigley, Burton, Weed—and Paschall. As they passed the door, going on to

Duval's desk, they were hard-faced. They usually remained, or pretended to remain, genial, casual, no
matter what happened. But not now. Next to suicides,
attempted escapes by force were what they feared and
disliked most. The particular doctors who had come
with Pot-Belly keyed it, so that I wasn't surprised
when Paschall appeared in the doorway and motioned
me. He didn't speak. I followed at his heels down to
my bedroom. He shut the door, and said:

"Did you do it?"

"No."

"Well, I knew you didn't, but Quigley thought perhaps you did. That's that. You can forget it. Hayden
[that was Pot-Belly] didn't think so, but we wanted
to clear this first. You can go on back to the smoking
room."

Spike had been pretty smart, I thought, but he had
missed out on the rest of his guesses. Nothing happened for a few minutes, and then we were all completely surprised, when Hayden himself came in and
asked Mr. Showalter and young Van Schaar to step
into the hall. I think they were among the last two
Spike or anybody else would have suspected. Showalter was one of the serious contract players, a suave
professor of music from some little university upstate,

who had committed himself voluntarily following a nervous breakdown, who had been there, always on the front halls, for nearly a year, and who, at least we thought, was going to be sent home any day now, discharged as cured. As for Van Schaar, he was a commonplace kid, rather dull, docile, not yet twenty, who had been committed by his mother, and with a lot of women-folks, aunts, older sisters, who came to see him twice a week and held long confabs about his diet and underwear with Mr. Duval.

Whatever the doctors had on those two was not behavioristic, and was completely unknown to us, their fellow-patients, but it must have been pretty strong, for they didn't come back to the smoking room. Nor was there any packing up. They were hustled back down to barred Hall Four, with only their pajamas and tooth brushes, for "observation." Their belongings followed next day.

The episode had a queer ending. Showalter came back in a couple of days, exonerated, unresentful, and told us why he had been suspected. In the previous week, he had had a serious disagreement with his doctor. He had felt he was ready to be sent home. His doctor had insisted that he remain a month longer. He had written a letter, in a temper, to his wife, and she, worried, had felt it her duty to report the letter. Showalter said he had meant court procedure, but the letter had been so worded, hastily, that it might have meant he was going to try to escape. He was self-committed, but self-commitment is no easier to abrogate than if others have committed you. So much for Showalter. It was the younger, more innocuous Van Schaar who had done it. He had confessed. We were a little longer learning the details of that. He had tried to escape from the high window with knotted bed-sheets, but it hadn't been precisely the "hospital" that he had wanted to escape from. He had been trying to escape from his mother, aunts and sisters! He had meant to run away and join the navy. His father was dead, he had no brothers, and the women at home, who still wanted to treat him as if he were nine years old, had been "driving him crazy," he said, for a long time. A while later—I imagine the psychiatrists must have done some missionary work on those women—the kid was taken out of our institution and sent to an Annapolis prep school.

IX

M Y INCLUSION as a suspect in the attempted window escape made me like Hall Two better and feel more at home there. This sounds like sheer perversity but the transitional elements were natural. "Papa" Duval, for instance, who had been sure I had a hand in it, went out of his way now to be a little more agreeable, as perhaps did fellow-patients. I began to play contract, listen to symphonies on the radio, even tried to learn to shoot bottle pool—in short, stopped beefing and sulking. "Everything," says Epictetus, "has two handles; one by which it can be carried, and one by which it cannot." I took hold now by the other handle, and carried on. Spike was already with us; a week or so later Johnny Reiss and Hauser were moved up, and we began to have a fairly good time.

Then, early in March, one afternoon at twilight, rather suddenly, deprived of drink for about three months, I developed a new set of symptoms, perhaps entered a new phase of gradual cure:

It was snowing outside the big windows; it was peaceful and warm inside; I was listening to muted Siegfried and Valhalla motifs—symphonic Rheingold excerpts coming from Carnegie Hall, tuned low on the radio—this may have been the fortuitous trigger— when I began to find myself interiorly illumined with a sort of mystical, if not maudlin, exaltation strangely like that which comes sometimes from prolonged drinking when the whiskey is good and one drinks a lot of it without becoming violent or sick. I suddenly found it wonderful, strange and beautiful, to be sober, and it curiously produced an illuminated sensitiveness which was astonishingly like the flashes a drunken man gets on the rare occasions when drunkenness seems golden and divine. It was as if a veil, or scum, or film had been stripped from all things visual and auditory, or as if the world had been suddenly diffused with a soft, unearthly, revealing light. I was sitting close to the radio, and was almost afraid to lift my head or move, for fear it all would fade. The colors in the carpet at my feet were abnormally vivid and made harmony. Mr. Duval came, standing in the doorway, and was looking in, as he did from time to time. I had seen him often thus, a fat-faced, fussy, spying, prying, pompously masculine old maid. I saw him now, benevolent, kindly and solicitous. He was my father and

mother. He wouldn't let me hurt myself or let anything hurt me. He was there to protect us, watch over
us, and be kind to us. Four or five fellow-patients were
scattered round the big room. I looked at their faces.
Their faces too were diffused with kindly, human
light—even the face of one I had disliked, now won-
dering why, for he was now my brother. Some minutes
had passed, but the illusion still persisted. It had not
flashed, fleeting. It was still there. I took stock of it.
I realized that it was wonderful and at the same time
slightly maudlin. I said to myself that if Quigley came
in at the moment, with his ugly, little, mean, pinched
face pursed in authority, I'd probably love him. I
didn't like that idea. I got up and shook myself, as it
were, walked over to the window. But the big, bare
trees against the white snow in the falling darkness
seemed of an unearthly, almost holy beauty. The thing
still persisted. I felt mildness and goodness and child-
like wonder within myself.

I said, "Tripe!" to myself. I said, "I might as well
be drunk." Instead of being pleased I shook myself
again and fought it, as one fights the waves of alcoholic intoxication. I thought, "This is the hooey. This
is a lot of baloney." I went out to the lavatory to wash
my face for supper.

At supper, I scarcely noticed my companions or Mr.

Duval. I was absorbed, not knowing whether to be pleased or not, with a further phase of what I began to think might be an authentic "mystical illumination," if it weren't just a maudlin neurasthenia caused by the shut-down on the large quantities of booze in which my system had been soaked. The phase was that dry, fresh bread, a piece of boiled potato, even the water, but particularly a scrap of plain, unbuttered bread, had a taste that was ridiculously delicious, heavenly. There was a breaded chop in tomato sauce, which I am usually fond of, and I cut a mouthful anticipating that since dry bread suddenly tasted like ambrosia, this now would taste better than any banquet a starving man had ever dreamed of. But I had guessed wrong. It seemed too highly seasoned—a mixed gambit of savors, too sharply seasoned. I said:

"Spike, was there too much salt and pepper on your chop, or does the tomato sauce seem sharp?"

"No," he said. "It's all right. I just put a little more salt on it."

So I knew its seeming too highly seasoned was a part of the weird state I was in. I got the same reaction to the salad dressing, but some leaves of lettuce with no dressing were as good to me as they would have been to a rabbit. And I still felt good and happy, though slightly scornful and puzzled about it.

I repeat that it was wonderful. It glowed benignly, like the precisely right amount of hashish, the third pipe of opium, the ninth glass of still champagne. I hoped I was drunk on sobriety. They had said it would take at least three months to get my alcohol-soaked tissues, nerves, organs and senses unpickled. I hoped it was that. I hoped I was seeing clear because I had been "purified," or some such nonsense. But I suspected that such an implied state of grace was too good to be true. To be drunk on sobriety would be turning earth into heaven, myself into a sort of saint, which, given what a rotten world it really is and what a marred, all-too-human hog I knew myself to be, was a reductio ad absurdum. More likely, some inherent neurasthenia, long drowned in gin, was now asserting itself. More likely I was "elated," which is a pleasant, agreeable term in common parlance, but means something not nearly so nice in technical psychiatric jargon.

But since it was so pleasant, as well as puzzling, I decided to let it ride, that is, to stop trying to rationalize it, stop trying to throw it off, let it lull me along to see where it led.

Lying in bed with the lights out, a new feeling came over me about the place I was in, about the institution. Since it was an emotional state rather than a process of reasoning, I may not now be able to describe it in

reasoned words. But it was as if I felt some of the following things, rather than catalogued or thought
them:

"I am in a safe sanctuary, surrounded by protec-
tions, by kindly companions, by devoted servants who
give me all things that are good for me and protect me
from things that would hurt me. Wise and kindly
superiors who wish me well, watch over all this with
benign power. All this is bestowed on me by day and
night, is 'given' me, requiring no effort, payment,
money or responsibility. My pockets are empty. I have
no money here. I need none. Here all things are free
as salvation. I am saved. No more fear and struggle.
I am safe in the arms of . . ."

It was precisely at this point of feeling, at this point
in letting things ride, that my thinking mind insisted
on shaking itself, sharpening the focus, impatient, and
suspicious:

"Safe in the arms of *what?*"

Safe in the arms of Papa Duval! Safe in the arms
of the psychiatrists! God forbid! Safe in the arms of
Jesus? Safe in the arms of my mother? Yes, I thought,
it had felt a little like that, like having been badly
hurt and being safe, soothed, protected, in my mother's
arms. But the old hymn-tune Jesus-phrase had sug-

gested another angle. I suddenly realized that in the factual history of my actual clinical case there had been a strong parallel, a striking analogy at any rate, with the mystical process of salvation as doctrinally outlined by the Christian church. At a given moment, I had "repented" in considerable fear and terror. I had known I was "lost" and wanted to be "saved." I had known that my own strength, my own will, could no longer save me. At the last, I had begged, screamed, pleaded to be "saved." I had been willing to "abase" myself, to relinquish myself, my life, my will, my body into hands stronger than my own. I was through, and I knew it, so far as any effort to save myself was concerned. I was stripped down, naked, to one thing only, which was the one and only thing the Church Fathers doctrinally recommend, *the desire for salvation.*

I had become an excellent candidate for the mourners' bench had my trouble been a soul rotten with sin instead of a belly rotten with whiskey, and maybe being in that stripped state had made me a more hopeful candidate than most for the different brand of salvation purveyed by the doctors and psychiatrists.

I am including all this now, as a part of the reportorial record of what happens to a drunkard who seeks serious, modern, scientific, medical-psychiatric aid to be cured, because I am convinced that it is all a part of what any man who has been a hard drinker for years must go through to come out of it. It is no joke. It involves going through strange stages, some pleasant, some painful. It cannot be done in a few weeks or a couple of months. I am not going by my own case alone. There are plenty of authoritative statistics. It is a hell of an adventure, and it takes the best part of a year or longer.

This present stage, which came after I had been deprived of drink for some three months, and which continued for several days, was strange but pleasant.

For instance, when I awoke the next morning, I was glad to be awake, and I was glad to put on my shirt. Some readers will know what that means, and some not. For so long that I couldn't remember, I had been awakening in the morning not caring whether I put on my shirt or not.

I told Paschall all about this new phase, and he didn't like it any too well. He felt there was some hidden cowardice in it. He was afraid I was turning chameleon, becoming institutionalized, too grateful and dependent on imprisonment, afraid I was still in love with the womb or the grave, and loved being locked up as a substitute for being dead—that is being afraid to face life. That afternoon—your all-round psychiatrist today regards psychoanalysis as just one useful instrument among many, rather than as the whole bag of tricks—he laid me on an easy couch after luncheon and tried what might spill out of my subconscious. I didn't do very well. I said dreamily that anyway I still thought Quigley was a son of a bitch, and he kept interrupting this and other reflections to reëxplain that he wanted me to try to talk without thinking anything, and I rambled for an hour or so, jumbling without thinking anything.

Months afterwards, he showed me this, which he had jotted down, he said, because, he said, it was significant:

". . . *when the coyote ran and chased in the baboon ditch the muddiest water before he was shut up in the asylum or the gas-house district before he was born or thought of being born while the red fox ran over the hill and so far away swift running little beast or beast when we go to the end of the said time we will find that their house has caught on fire before the people came and went away from this place in the old days before the war and he turned out to be a hound and Mary.*"

This was in midsummer, just before they turned me out. He let me copy it, but said:

"You'd better not put that in if you write anything about yourself."

"Why not?"

"Well, it's too much of a give-away," he replied with a grin.

At the actual time when this occurred, he had merely told me that I'd probably go through a period of depression next, and not to worry too much about it when it came. That, he said, would be the "hang-over." But all the rest of that week, the pleasant glow persisted from day to day. I still awakened every morning glad to put on my shirt, and found a mild spontaneous delight in all things. I had previously begun to like things pretty well, but this was different. About working in the shop, making a new chair, for instance. Up to now, I had made myself like it, sincerely, but now I took spontaneous pleasure in it, in the tools, in the grain and texture of the seasoned oak under the fine edge of the plane or chisel.

It was on Monday that a little accident occurred in the carpenter shop which had no serious consequences except that it—or rather the consequences it threatened to have—knocked my maudlin, elation-intoxicated moonings for a goal. In the morning, I pressed down too hard with the drawknife on a curved piece of chair-back I was shaping. It flew out of the vise and gashed me above the eye, a harmless little gash, but in a conspicuous place and naturally a little bloody, and the outcome of it was that Dr. Quigley nearly succeeded in railroading me out of the carpenter shop, into the basket-weaving department with the doddering old gentlemen and suicidal patients.

If Joe, our foreman, and afterward Paschall, hadn't helped me crook it, Quigley would certainly have succeeded. The rules would have justified him, because if a patient hurts himself with tools, intentionally or unintentionally, he is shifted for a while to a safer shop, and it wouldn't have been human if Quigley had dealt any way but by rule of thumb with me, for I was consistently and openly as nasty to him as I could be at all times.

Of course, Joe knew all this—everybody always knew everything in our tangled, restricted little world —and liked me because I was an enthusiastic learner, also because he could talk with me of Leeds and London when he was homesick. No patient had chanced to see the accident. Joe snaked me to a closet and said, "That wood's clean, not a chance in a thousand of infection, let's take a little chance on it." So instead of iodine and a bandage, he washed it, dabbed it with alum, put "new-skin"—collodion—over it instead of court plaster, and then touched it up with some gray, powdered soapstone which was the nearest thing he had to make-up or talcum powder. There was a mirror there. It looked queer, phony, if you stared straight at it, but it wasn't conspicuous. It didn't leap out and catch the eye. We went back into the shop and when the bell rang I got past Purdy and the people at the door, and over into the gymnasium with the rest of the crowd without it being noticed. I said I wasn't feeling up to volley ball and went downstairs to the bowling alleys, kept out of the bright light as much as possible, my cap pulled down when we returned to our hall, so that nobody noticed it at all until at luncheon Papa Duval inevitably spied it.

All physical injuries to patients, no matter how inconsequential, must be immediately put down on the chart and reported, so after luncheon Papa Duval wanted to know all about it.

I assured him it was nothing at all, that I had merely bumped my head a little in the gymnasium. Yes, but what had been done to it? He made me sit

down so that he could study it, with increasing suspicion. Wasn't it cut underneath? And no iodine! Who
had put that "new-skin" on it?

Oh, one of the fellows, one of Tim's helpers at the
gymnasium.

Which one?

I didn't remember.

He knew I was lying, of course. And he knew what
to do. He took me into the treatment room, stripped
all the collodion off, gently, but it bled a little, dabbed
it more than was necessary with iodine, and fixed it up
with a patch of dressing held by criss-cross strips of
adhesive tape, so that anybody could see it a mile, and
so that everybody who saw me from then on said:

"Gee, fellow, how'd you cut your face?"

Quigley was portentous and made me lie to him,
which I did surlily, but not well.

That night Paschall removed Papa Duval's bill-
board and replaced it with a small strip of court
plaster.

"It's nothing, but you'd better come clean about
how you did it."

"Why, didn't Mr. Duval tell you? I thought he
put it on the chart. Bumped my head in the gymnasium."

"Listen, Dr. Quigley's seen the chart. He's seen

Timothy Devlin too, and all the gymnasium attendants. He knows you didn't do it in the gymnasium."

"All right," I said, "if he insists. I did it trying to
climb over the fence, or I had a fight with Charlie
Logan, or one of the attendants hit me and I don't
want to make him lose his job by reporting it because
he is taking care of a crippled mother, or . . ."

"You didn't by any chance do it in the carpenter
shop, did you?" he interrupted.

"You know I did it in the carpenter shop," I said.
"You know that's the point, but please cover me on it,
won't you? As a favor. I'll swear I did it any way you
like, except in the carpenter shop. Can't you fix it for
me?"

"I can't do anything about it," he said, "but you
seem to have been pretty smart about it. Purdy didn't
notice anything when you checked out of the Occupation Building, and if Joe lied, he'll have to stick to it
for his own sake. If whoever helped you doesn't spill
it, I don't see how we can pin anything on you."

"Thank you very much," I said. "You're pretty
swell; you always have been swell to me, but this
dump is beginning to get on my nerves."

Marjorie says that when she brought me grapes that
Wednesday, she was more worried than any time since

the first few weeks. She said I looked depressed, nervous, unhappy. She says I told her that Quigley was persecuting me, that the whole atmosphere of the place was petty, that it had been a mistake to send me here, that I was sick of it, and that as for being cured I had made no progress whatever.

X

FAVORITE thesis among us, when we were out of humor or fed up, was that psychiatry smells of baloney, that all psychiatrists are nuts. They often seemed so.

Paschall, for instance, assured me now that I was doing much better, improving, because I felt awful! Since I loathed the dump, was sore again at everybody, had the blues and was convinced the three months' treatment had done me no good at all, he was sure I was getting better!

He had a hard time convincing me of this, and an even harder time convincing Marjorie, who went to him a couple of successive afternoons in tears and had lost her nerve again about this being a wholesome place for me.

Paschall insisted that the paradox was true—that it would have been unwholesome if I had remained in love with it. The hospital already had a queer little group of "trusties," less than half a dozen, who could get their discharge papers and walk out free any day they liked, but who probably would never go. They were happy here, no longer "mentally disturbed," but they had lost the courage, or the wish, to face the world outside. One was an elderly commercial artist who worked regularly at his drawing board and sold his stuff through a New York agent; one was a former laundryman who had been here nine years now, by his own volition, after the doctors had pronounced him cured, working in the asylum, submitting to all the restrictions, including being locked up every night, because he preferred it to living on his own responsibility outside. It was his own affair. But less pleasant was the case of Mr. Drummond, a silk merchant in a big way who had crashed in 1929 and gone to pieces. He had been put together again, but his wife, who had once had five servants, a box at the opera and three cars, now peddled embroidery to her former friends, because her once-rich husband hadn't the guts to go out and begin life again as a poor man. Monastery, prison, hospital, nursery, it sheltered us from the hard, stormy world; it kept us from the foggy, foggy dew.

It had been a heaven and haven for me because I had been drenched and drowning, but it would be just too bad if, because of that, I never dared to go out in the rain again.

I guessed, morosely, that Paschall had been right,

and when next we talked I told him so. He ended by pretty well proving there was a streak of coward, quitter, in me somewhere; tired and frightened, I had run back to mamma. A padded cell, hospital, nursery, the grave—all different names for mother's protecting arms— "By the way," Paschall demanded casually, "did you ever consider suicide as a solution?"

"No," I told him truly, "but when I passed cemeteries I often thought how peaceful and beautiful they were and was sometimes in love with the idea of being dead."

"All fear," he said, "all based on fear. You probably drank because you were afraid of something. You probably became a drunkard because there was something you were afraid to face sober."

It made me sore, but we had a long talk about it. And out popped another pretty notion of his, to wit, that I was still unconsciously afraid of something— other than whiskey—and that consequently my "mystical illumination" had been a wish-trick toward "escape by imprisonment," that is, a wish to give up and stay here always.

This had made me even sorer, but I remembered how silly a fellow patient named Jake Eckstein had seemed to me when he had gone into hysterical rage because his psychoanalyst had asked him *why* he had

wanted to kill his father. Jake was a self-made Ghetto
Jew who had learned law at City College without
learning much of anything else. He had never heard
of Oedipus, Havelock Ellis or D. H. Lawrence. I
doubt if he had ever heard of Dr. Freud, or the stock
commonplaces of the new psychology. I mean, every
callow sophomore these days is familiar and bored
with the idea that he was in love with his mother and
wanted to murder the old man. But to Jake, the idea
had been astounding, unspeakable. I remembered how
we had heard him screaming at the doctor all the way
down the hall through the closed door of his bedroom:

"Why, you wicked degenerate monster! To put
such a horrible thought as that into my head!"

Spike had whispered to me afterward, when we
heard it all from the outraged Jake himself:

"It's lucky the doctor didn't tax him too with being
in love with his mamma, or we'd have had bloody
murder right here on the floor."

It occurred to me now that I didn't want to be as
naïve as Jake. I decided, after Paschall had left me,
that instead of getting mad about it I would think it
over. One of the things about being locked up for a
long time is that, despite workshops and gymnasium,
it gives you plenty of time to think.

I want to set down briefly some of the things I

thought, not because I consider myself a unique or specially interesting individual, but because, on the contrary, I may be a quite common or flourishing, weedy garden variety of the white-collared, educated drunkard—and a legitimate general interest may lie in that.

My first thoughts were physiological. I thought about how I had enjoyed believing that I was the victim of some glandular, stomach or nervous craving for alcohol, and that three months of incarceration during which I had been given no medicine or drugs whatever, had already exploded that alibi. It had been a false excuse. Once finished with my prolonged hangover and jitters, I had never felt any physiological craving at all. I slept well and ate well. My nerves had been shot to pieces *by* the liquor, and I had perhaps been forced to increase the doses, but now that I drank no liquor at all, my nerves were all right. So adieu to that alibi.

Why, then, with a nice home, easy living, money in bank, an agreeable occupation, a lovely lady, and good friends, had I become a drunkard at all?

Paschall insisted it had been because I was afraid of something. Very well. Afraid of what?

Presently, not suddenly, but slowly, not liking it, I knew:

I was afraid I wasn't good enough. Always had been afraid, but maybe in youth believed age would remedy it. Now I was middle-aged and afraid I'd never be good enough.

I imagine this is a fairly common ailment, a fairly common worry, a fairly common fear. My trade happens to be that of a writer, but I suspect all trades are pretty much the same. A man hopes to do well at his trade, and doesn't do as well as he had hoped, and begins, after blaming other things, to doubt his own ability, begins to be afraid he hasn't got it. I don't see why this shouldn't be the same in all trades, and I doubt whether seeming success, comparative real success, or failure has much bearing on it. I have known middle-aged grocery clerks on small salaries in little stores who are competent, cheerful, self-reliant. They have no fear that they are not good enough, because they are good enough—very good at what they are satisfied to do. But I wonder, for instance, whether many a little millionaire is afraid he isn't good enough when he thinks of Morgan; I wonder what Rudy Vallee thinks when he thinks of Toscanini; I wonder what Toscanini thinks when he thinks of Beethoven. Maybe Toscanini thinks, "I'm a little brass monkey with a baton; I would give my soul to suffer and write a great symphony." Of course, probably he doesn't. But I don't see how success helps if one has the neurasthenic temperament. I hear Gershwin in person on the radio, doing marvelously good stuff, sounding happy, lime-lighted, complimented, richly paid for it, and wonder whether Gershwin ever thinks of Rimsky-Korsakov. I wonder, if he did, often, whether he would take to drink. I wonder, likewise, whether Rimsky-Korsakov is still poor and neglected in Tiflis and perhaps thinks of Gershwin.[1] I wonder whether Fannie Hurst some-times thinks of Virginia Woolf and whether Virginia Woolf ever thinks of Fannie Hurst. Might either or both of them be tempted to drown themselves in gin if they thought too much about each other? Not prob-ably, not any of them, unless they were cowardly or neurasthenic in worrying about whether they were "good enough" in one different way or another.

Well, common or not, what I was afraid of was that I wasn't good enough, and cowardly-neurasthenic or not, I was about ready to admit that this was why I had tried to drown myself in booze. Good enough for precisely what? Well, it wasn't complicated, and I am not ashamed to admit it, for it was not too pretentious.

---

[1] AUTHOR'S NOTE: I have learned since writing this that Rimsky-Korsakov is dead.

It did not involve wanting to be Shakespeare or Joyce. What I wanted more than anything was simply to be a good writer, and what I was afraid of was that I would never be anything at most but a good reporter.

Admitting this fear, why had I tried to drown it in the particular period of 1932 and 1933? Because I had reached middle age? Or because "nothing fails like success"? By which I merely mean that my writing, whether good, bad or mediocre, had been published by good publishers, had made a quantity of money, and that prosperity is poison to some people. These things had been elements in it, but they hadn't been the main thing. The main thing had been the cowardice which had come to a head in 1932 and 1933 because I had been caught in a trap. I had made and baited and walked into the trap myself. It had consisted of perfect—for me—surroundings and conditions under which to live and work, plus ample material of the precise sort I wanted, assembled and waiting to be worked on. I had good contracts, no rush, no money worries, good health and good intentions. There had been time, opportunity, material, to do my best. There had been no loophole for subsequent alibis, no place to run away to, because I was already where I wanted to be—and instead of doing my best I took to drink and did practically nothing. I had been afraid to do my best for fear my best would not be good enough.

A man stalls, loafs, procrastinates, sits in cafés, fails to throw all his best energy into a piece of work. He cannot bring himself to put "everything" into it, to "do his damnedest," as the saying goes. Accused or self-accused of being lazy, he confesses—to laziness. But he doesn't confess that he is afraid of destroying forever the illusion that he may some day ring the bell.

I knew now that I had always been afraid of a showdown. I saw now that I had been running away all my life. I had been variously listed and publicized as an "explorer," "traveler," "adventurer," but I had always been merely a frightened man running away— from something. It had begun a quarter of a century before, soon after I had quit college. At twenty-one I had been city editor of the Augusta (Georgia) *Chronicle*, had stood it for six months and thrown it up to be a tramp in Southern Europe. Returning, a few years later, I had been established on the Atlanta *Journal*, then later with a partnership interest in an advertising agency and a directorship in the then new Atlanta Rotary Club. In 1915 I had chucked it all and run away again. I had run away to war like the

Spoon River soldier, not caring who won it, caring little indeed, since we were then neutral, which side I joined. I had come back, a little gassed but not badly, started farming in Georgia, and ran away from that as soon as I had cleared the land and planted the first crop. When the crop came up, if it ever did, I was working for City Editor Phillips of the New York *Times* as a $27.50 a week reporter. In 1924, making more money than I needed in soft jobs with the syndicates, I got sick of it, met an Arab, and ran away into the Arabian desert where I joined a tribe and got along so well that its sheikh offered me an oasis village on the edge of Transjordania, a hundred men and a couple of new wives, including his niece. I ran away again, and this time kept running, all over the map, for miles and years (with books as by-products of my circlings) until I got caught in a trap of my own devising where I had to sit down and face myself and do my utmost. I had been so unwilling and afraid to face it that I had tried to drown myself in booze. I had been forced at last to stop running and sit down with myself—and it had landed me—by the back door, since I hadn't even the excuse of being cracked—in this place.

Well, I thought, I had plenty of time to face myself

now, and if I wanted to come out and survive, I had
to take stock of whatever I was and get the courage to
face it without trying to drown the image in drink
again. I had to stop running away from myself, I had
to stop hiding from myself, I had to stop drowning
myself in gin. Whatever I had was all I had, and if I
weren't a hopeless coward, I had to do my best with
what I had. It made me sick. I loathed people who
thought or talked about themselves or others in such
copy-book, cabbage-patch jargon. I didn't think I had
ever thought in such terms before. Well, maybe I
needed a good dose of homely, banal, moral twaddle
to balance me. God knows I had swung far enough in
dervish directions.

When I spilled all this, and more, to Paschall, he
agreed that we'd probably arrived at the reason behind
my prolonged heavy drinking and smash-up. Knowing
it, he warned me, didn't necessarily mean I was cured
of it or free of it. He said the popular notion that
twists, complexes, neurasthenic quirks could be got rid
of by merely trotting them out into the daylight was all
poppycock, psychoanalytic superstition. He hoped I
might be happier now that I knew and admitted what
was basically the matter with me, but said the main
thing they hoped to do was simply to break me perma-

nently from the habit of using alcohol as a psychic-pain-killer, as an anesthetic, as a coward's-refuge, and that he hoped to goodness I'd reconcile myself to remaining locked up long enough to do that, for he believed they could do it, and remarked that even if it didn't make me any happier it would, at any rate, be something.

"I'll be honest in telling you that the main thing now is time," he added—"just a matter of patience and sticking it out. Don't fool yourself that you're cured yet, and don't expect any sudden miracles. They don't occur in cases of your sort."

Miracles did occur from time to time in queerer cases, and I guessed he had in mind the recent miracle of Dr. Rowland, which had occurred somewhat spectacularly before a cloud of witnesses in the gymnasium.

XI

W̲E ALL knew more or less everything there was to know about Dr. Rowland because his wife, who came twice a week, was a voluble, unembarrassed and by no means stupid woman who felt that her husband was the most important patient in the hospital and consequently the most interesting subject for conversation.

His case was interesting enough, and even if it hadn't been, we all liked Mrs. Rowland, and liked to hear her talk. She had trace of accent, like Irene Bordoni off stage. She wasn't young, but was still handsome. She was half American and half extremely upper-class Bucharest Roumanian, quite in the Queen Marie tradition. Her mother had been a princess of the Holy Roman Empire, and it may have been her blood which made her take it for granted that she could treat anybody and everybody *sans façon*. Hers was a sort of snobbery, but the diametric opposite of American snobbery. She smoked cigarettes with the

nurses, swore at the doctors, swapped appalling inti-
macies with all of us, and rode in the front seat with
her chauffeur.

Her husband had been in the asylum for more than
a year, and she was beginning to be fed up and annoyed by it, though loyal and deeply concerned. He
was all-American, but of Teutonic stock, a research
chemist high up in some German-American dye com-
bine until he had tried to hang himself, nobody knew
quite why, and had afterward sunken into manic-
depressive gloom, with the accent all on the depressive.

None of us knew whether we liked Dr. Rowland or
not. It was hard to have any feeling toward him except to be sorry for him. We all knew him, in a manner of speaking, for he had gone the rounds of all the
halls—had been in and out of Four a couple of times
during my sojourn. The doctors switched him around,
sometimes almost at random, I think, in the hope he'd
hit on something to "change his ideas," to cheer him
up. For he generally just sat, or moved, sunken, staring, in awful, silent misery. The doctors knew what
was the matter with him, if not the why of it. He had
a horrid, pathological case of self-hatred, self-condem-
nation, self-loathing. He had never committed any
shameful crime—he was the victim of some insane

hallucination—but his state was similar to that which a sane man's might be if he had murdered babies and kittens, or had cut his mother's head off and thrown it to the pigs. He felt that he was too vile, too low, to live. The first pragmatic step, therefore, toward his possible cure, was to cheer him up a little, and this might be brought about by some chance word spoken, or thing done, by a nurse or fellow-patient—as likely it might happen that way as through anything done by the doctors. This was doubtless one of the reasons why Mrs. Rowland was always talking with us about her husband, urging us to notice him, to try to draw him into talk or play, to try to cheer him up. She would inquire among all of us each time she came whether he had shown any signs of interest that might be encouraging. We often tried, but it would have been easier to cheer a deaf, dumb and blind man suffering from cancer. He was pretty bad. The old sort of asylum, I'm sure, would have let him sit in a corner in his horrid gloom. He wouldn't have been in a cell, for he was never violent, but I'm sure he wouldn't have been dragged around. Here, employing the new psychiatry, they shunted and dragged him around continually—made him go to the workshops with us though he only sat and stared at the old men weaving baskets, made him go to the gymnasium though he only stood and stared at the rest of us taking exercise, or more often merely stood with sunken head staring at the floor or nothing.

Then, some time in February, he began at intervals to stare at Daly. This Daly was a young welterweight who had been in the ring before he went crazy. He was now on one of the back halls, and was brought over every couple of days to the gymnasium to punch the bag. This was in a far corner of the cage upstairs where we played volley ball. He would punch the bag, expertly, for half hours at a time, rhythmically, tattooing it with lightning-rapid taps, interspersed with powerful, equally rhythmic hooks and smashes.

We all knew that the punching bag had caught Dr. Rowland's attention; it was reported likewise to the doctors, to his wife when next she came; and we all speculated about it. Paschall told me they were afraid it had no significance—that in all probability he was merely watching it hypnotically, as a cat stares at a swinging pendulum, or a baby at a whirligig. But whatever it was, day after day, Dr. Rowland stared gloomily at Daly and the punching bag instead of at the floor.

Then, one day, he plucked an attendant's sleeve and

asked who Daly was. This was astonishing and was also duly reported, since it was the first question Rowland had asked during his whole long stay in the asylum, but no special significance was seen in it other than the encouraging fact that he had evinced an interest, if ever so slight, in *something*.

The attendant, who happened to be Dan, was an addict of the sporting pages, and had been able to give Rowland a detailed sketch of Daly's ring career. Daly had once gone six rounds with Ted Lewis, had knocked out so-and-so in Buffalo, had won a decision over some nigger or other in New Orleans, etc. How much Rowland had understood of this there had been no way to guess, but Dan had told him all he could.

Well, next day the attendants were watching our volley ball game as usual, some of them playing with us, while Daly was at his punching bag over in the isolated corner, with Rowland, as usual, standing some ten feet away from Daly, staring. The two were all by themselves over there. No need for any guard to be near them. Daly had never been known to swing at anything except the bag and Rowland was always physically docile as a sick cow. He was a gray-faced man, nearing sixty, of medium stature, flabby. Daly paused in a perspiration, stepped away from the bag for a moment's breathing spell, and was half turned toward Rowland. Rowland stepped briskly forward, slapped Daly's astonished face a quick, staccato but harmless wham, then dropped his hands and stood open-mouthed with his chin lifted and his head poked slightly forward as children do when a friendly family doctor says, "Let me look at your tongue." Daly's mechanical reaction—like a mechanical toy when the spring is touched—was an almost simultaneous right hook to Rowland's jaw. His elbow had been bent, his fist had scarcely moved ten inches, but his whole shoulder had been behind it. Rowland lay cold on the floor and Daly stood there in helpless, dazed surprise, as Timothy and four attendants rushed toward them. They didn't pounce on Daly, who stood like a statue, his face expressing nothing but mild wonder. They busied themselves with Rowland who was already opening his eyes.

"He asked for it!" Casey was whispering to Tim. "Jesus! Did you see him ask for it? He went over and asked for it like you'd ask somebody to pass the salt!"

Rowland, whose open eyes began to look less glassy, now opened his mouth too and said dreamily:

"Yes, I asked for it. I thought it might do me a lot of good."

Timothy in the meantime had been feeling his jaw, and there was nothing broken, no harm done. The tension was relieved, and Casey, whose first comment had been awe-stricken, got up from where he had been kneeling, grinned, and said:

"Well, you certainly got it, Dr. Rowland. Did it make you feel any better?"

Whereupon Dr. Rowland, who now had a pillow under his head and had been given a drink of water, smiled a faint smile—the first ghost of a smile any of us had ever seen on his lost-soul's face, and said cheerfully:

"Yes, I think it did."

Believe it or not, as Ripley says, Rowland began from then on to come out of it. He began to take an interest in things and to coöperate. Before a week had passed he was saying good morning grouchily and reading the newspapers. The psychiatrists were delighted, if somewhat taken aback. Mrs. Rowland was a scream. She sent Daly a box of candy, and said to Spike:

"You know . . . these last months . . . I've often wanted to do it myself."

The Rowland miracle in the gymnasium was our best miracle, certainly our most spectacular during my residence in this realm of psychiatric voodoo, but we had others from time to time which, if less violent, were equally veritable. The unpredictable nature of the happening through which the cleansing flame might descend made me wonder sometimes whether a major element in psychiatry might not be simply a matter of supplying the patient with safe, pleasant surroundings, and then waiting for something to happen.

In this apparent category was the strange case of Willie Bronson, who had been in one of the sick-rooms on Hall Four when I arrived in December. He was a man of perhaps fifty-five, a leading citizen of one of the biggest cities in the Middle West. He and his brothers had been, still are, among its feudal bosses—business and social barons in their twentieth century Verona with irons in every fire; banks, clubs, politics, symphony series and senatorial elections, expending vast amounts of energy on myriad tangled activities— and this middle brother, Willie, it seemed, had been the driving force, the star, the most rushed and tangled of them all—until he cracked. Cracked isn't exactly the word. "He had flatted, like a tire," said one of his brothers who came in a big car, every couple of weeks or so, half way across the continent, to see him. "Not like a blow-out—more like a good tire that had been punctured or had a leaky valve." So they had sent him here to be mended. When he had first been brought in, so Miss Pine told me, several months prior to my own arrival, they had had to feed him with a spoon. He hadn't been manic-depressed or melancholy. He hadn't even been depressed. He hadn't been anything. He had been like an idiot baby, Miss Pine said. When I first saw him, he was more like a robot or a zombie. They had begun to make him dress every day, eat at table, go to walk, go regularly with the rest of us over to the workshops where his hands wove baskets, but he never spoke, never uttered a sound of any sort, never smoked, never looked at anyone, merely went through the mechanical motions of what he was forced to do, without showing the slightest sign of either pleasure or distaste. He apparently didn't even suffer. He was tall, long-legged, with a pointed nose, and he would sometimes spend hours standing, "like a goddamned hypnotized stork," as Spike put it, by the side of his made-up bed. He hadn't spoken a word of any sort, they said, since he had entered the institution.

One dark morning, with snow still on the ground, we had finished breakfast, finished our cigarettes, finished our newspapers, and were idling until the little man in the derby came to take us to the workshop. I have mentioned that little man before, telling how he always sang out "Occupation" in a nasal, bored voice which he seemed to be trying to inflect with a false, crooning mother's caress. He was just about due. The clock showed twenty-nine minutes or so after eight, and he always appeared on the stroke of eight-thirty. Our Willie, as usual, was standing in a lonely corner with his head dropped to one side, exactly, as Spike had said, like an elderly stork in a dream. Hall Four was on the ground floor, and the man in the derby passed, crossing the path, outside our own bay window. Then we heard his key in the door, but before the door opened we heard also, suddenly, prematurely, from the wrong, opposite direction—from the direction of Willie's lone corner—a sharp, nasal voice, bored and malicious, yet at the same time gleeful, lifted in cunning mimicry of the familiar, false-maternal croon:

"OCCU-PAY-SHAAUN!"

We turned as if the roof had fallen in, to stare at Willie. There was a guilty grin on his face, and his eyes which had hitherto been vacant as a sick baby's, had a keen, amused gleam.

The man in the derby had meanwhile opened the door to stand gaping, and turned a bewildered crimson as we roared with laughter. Willie was excused from the workshop and Dirk phoned the doctors. When we got back he had sent out for a box of Corona Coronas and was reading all the old newspapers Dirk could find. He had fired off a lot of telegrams with the help of the doctors, gave Miss Pine lessons in cheating at cards that night, and was transferred next day to one of the convalescent villas where he spent an amused, impatient month or two getting back his physical strength and playing billiards. In April we waved him good-by.

XII

BY LATE April the scene in our park had changed, buds were bursting, robins came, swings and benches were repainted, and the outdoor squad began to work on the tennis courts. By early May our tempo and routine changed too. The object seemed to be to keep us out of doors as much as possible among the blossoms, babbling brooks and butterflies. They turned us all outdoors—all the halls, including the wild ones—and while we were kept more or less in hall-groups under surveillance of attendants from our own respective halls, a certain amount of fraternizing was permitted, even encouraged. Thus, in time, I made new friends, and queer ones.

The lawns and rolling hills turned green, peach blossoms bloomed, squirrels made love, birds laid eggs, the gymnasium was closed except on rainy days, workshop hours were curtailed, the Daughters of Polonius waved to us through the high spiked fence that separated their park from ours, a certain Miss Doremus who had believed she was a mouse in the winter now proclaimed that she was the Scarlet Whore of Babylon, and Spike wanted to know how soon we could start playing golf.

"In a couple of weeks," replied Timothy, "but there'll be plenty of baseball in the meantime."

We had a full-sized ball field and diamond near the gym. I played second base occasionally later, but the first game of the season is the one I remember best. I remember three incidents in particular, of which the first was merely a scrap of conversation. A Californian we called Frankie who muttered a great deal and always seemed harassed by something, came in from the field at the end of an inning and sat on one of the benches near me. He had covered third base, assisting in a double-play, and I imagine Timothy or somebody had been complimenting him. At any rate, I heard him say:

"I don't know how I could have done it, for I was sending telegrams all the time."

The next diversion came from a player who, it turned out, had been on the receiving end of a wire, or maybe wireless. Imaginary telegrams, urgent spirit calls and astral admonitions came frequently to our home on the hill. This time it was a long-legged musical chap named Ewald, who lammed one into deep left field, and started down toward first at top speed while we cheered. It was going to be a three-bagger if not a home run. "Go on! Go on!" we shouted. Reaching first base, he went on all right, he kept going at top speed, but not toward second. He kept going in a continuing straight line, sprinting first, then covering the ground in leaps like a pursued antelope—toward the spiked iron boundary fence in the trees. The gym attendants followed like a pack of hounds on his heels, a hundred yards behind. We continued to cheer. A white-coat came running from beyond the woods, to cut him off. He had reached the fence and was climbing when they pulled him down. He made no resistance. They seemed to be talking amiably as they all strolled back, Ewald himself quite unperturbed, but hurrying toward Timothy he said:

"They didn't understand. I'm sorry but you'll have to excuse me from finishing the game. I have to go to Philadelphia. I had a phone call from Mr. Stokowski. We'd better go see about the trains."

"Shu-rr-r-e!" said Timothy, cordially, "we'll just go right along and see about them."

They went, a substitute was picked for Ewald and the game resumed.

The third episode occurred in a later inning. A spoiled rich baker's son from Brooklyn was pitching— a fat boy from one of the back halls, a bubbling, witty, half-wit type whom the attendants petted and kidded a lot. He pitched a fast, straight ball but the opposing team had caught onto it and was beginning to knock him out of the box, while his teammates began yelling to have him taken out. Whereupon, he wangled a less ignominious benching. He wound up, threw a wild one, leaped into the air and fell down screeching bloody murder.

"Aiee! Yi-yi-yi-yi! My arm's out of joint! I threw my arm out of joint! And my leg's broken!"

We crowded around while Casey felt him over, winking.

"All right. Get up, Bud. We'll put you to bed and put in another pitcher."

"I can't walk, Casey! I can't walk! I'll have to be carried!"

"Yeah, in a baby carriage! A fine pitcher you turned out to be! They knocked you all over the field, and you couldn't take it! You're not fooling anybody!"

Bud stopped screaming and pouted.

"Honest, Casey," he said, "I can't walk off the field. I'll have to be carried."

Spike suggested a stretcher. They improvised one
with a deck chair. Half way off the diamond, the re-
cumbent fat boy sat up, saluting the crowd, beaming
with triumph, bowing right and left like an emperor.

They dumped him on the grass, and he said:

"Casey, can I play in center field next inning?"

I mean nothing callous, heartless or inconsiderate in
retrospect when I say that when our various Halls
began to mingle and play together outdoors, we "en-
tertained each other." Aside from mingling more in
actual games and sports, tennis, croquet, pitching
horseshoes, ninepins, we learned more about each
other's idiosyncrasies, saw each other at the same time
more intimately yet with wider scope, occasionally
found ourselves shocked, pitying, sympathizing—but
much more frequently amused. Being all of us part of
it, companion unfortunates in similar case though for
wide dissimilarity of reasons, we laughed at each other
when things were funny, enjoyed each other's antics
and delusions without embarrassment or shame. For
instance, when a patient named Schriver mistook the
gardener's collie for a bloodhound and concluded that
they had a whole pack of them hidden in the base-
ments to chase us if we got past the fences—which he
believed were charged with high voltage electricity—

I'm afraid we didn't say, "Poor fellow, what a pity!"
We added masked machine-guns in the tower, and
played with the bloodhound idea for a week. I don't
mean, either, that Spike, myself, or the nearly-cured
patients of the convalescent villas—those of us un-
subject to hallucinations—were the only ones who
saw occasional humor in other men's delusions. Spike
and I, for instance, were sometimes mildly amused by
the delicatessen merchant who believed he was Napoleon Bonaparte, but the man who found it uproari-
ously funny was the one *who was sure he was Napoleon himself.*[1]

Patients who believed they were somebody else—
usually characters from history—had been rare on
Halls Four and Two, but now we became acquainted
with a number of them. There were the three Napoleons, one Julius Caesar, strangely a Unitarian minis-
ter who had switched sexes and believed he was Bla-
vatski, the artillery major who was sometimes a little
girl, the movie director who was Pontius Pilate. There
was an elderly gentleman we saw less of who believed
he was a rooster, and a little chap who said, "Tinkle,

[1] AUTHOR'S NOTE: This sounds like cheap vaudeville, but the Napoleon hallucination is one of the commonest. We had three
Napoleons.

tinkle, tinkle." He thought he was the bell inside a telephone.

How continuous these delusions were, or how intermittent, or to what extent some of the patients who had them knew they were delusions, it was difficult to judge. The gentleman who thought he was a rooster, for instance, played an excellent game of tennis, kept score accurately, but crowed when he made a particularly good shot. A problem in this category was one of the humming birds. A "humming bird" in the argot of the attendants, is a patient addicted to screaming, crying, howling when not in discomfort or pain. This particular one was a problem to the attendants as well as to his fellow-patients. He said to me once:

"You know, I have one of the hardest jobs in this hospital. When the rest of you sleep, I have to keep awake to yell when the late doctors come round."

He seldom did his stuff unless there was a doctor somewhere in the vicinity to hear him. His attendant confided to me that one night they had played a trick on him. He was sitting quiet one late afternoon in the hall when they told him that Dr. Cain had come into the corridor. Immediately he began to scream at the top of his lungs, but Dr. Cain failed to materialize. In a minute he stopped yelling, went out in the corridor and discovered that no doctor had come in at all. Returning quietly to his newspaper he said:

"Hell, you made me waste all that breath for nothing."

I want to defend myself, at this point, against a charge which I am sure my mother, for one, would make against me if she were still alive, to wit, that it is heartless and unkind to be amused, to "laugh" at anything a deranged person does or says, and that it is in even worse taste to make "copy" of it afterward. I have thought about this. I have gone into it with friends, and with my publisher who is a friend as well as publisher. My defense is that a good nine-tenths of the patients I describe, including some of the "wildest" ones with the most fantastic hallucinations, have already gone out of that institution, or will go out, cured and sane. In other words, that most forms of mental derangement have lost their element of hushed shame and horror-pity by the fact that modern psychiatry has proven them curable, and has shown them to be no more to be ashamed of than having been physically smashed up in a motor accident. I might add, if my mother were still dubious about the decency of these chapters, that while I have been completely personal about my own unpretty case, all other actual names and identities of other cases and characters have been so scrupulously, carefully deleted that no slightest hurt, guess or suspicion of identity can ever result from the publication of this to embarrass any former fellow-patient or any of their families. This being true, I may add that a good deal of the stuff that goes on in such an institution *is* funny, de facto, whether it ought to be or not, and that any picture which leaves it out would be sentimental buncombe.

If you will come along with me on that basis, it may not shock your sense of kindliness toward misfortune, or your sense of good taste either, when I tell you that not only we other patients, but the attendants and doctors as well, refused to take "Suicide Simpkins" seriously. His name wasn't Simpkins, of course. We had nicknamed him. And the nickname stuck despite the fact that suicide is the least funny of all possible subjects in an asylum. But it was not in cases like this man's that it needed to be taken seriously. He spent his time trying to annoy the attendants and frighten the rest of us. We had long since ceased to be frightened or annoyed. His conversations, adapted to what we might be doing, were generally on a par with his remarking loudly one day when we walked round the pond, "No, I won't drown myself today. The water is too muddy." Another day, it was too cold, and on still another day it was because there were muskrats in it. His frequent pantomimes were not heartrending. One day at the door of the golf house, first glancing around to make sure he had an audience, he seized the door, heaved mightily toward it with his shoulders, tapping his forehead lightly against it, but at the same time giving it a resounding surreptitious bang with his foot. He was continually staging scenes of that sort, but never gave himself the slightest bruise or scratch. He was a fair representative of a type of patient, of whom we had many, which convinced me that a man may be quite mad and at the same time a persistent comedian. One would guess that such patients had learned *Hamlet* by heart, or that Shakespeare had lived at some time in a madhouse. When the wind was fair, they worked overtime razzing the life out of the doctors, and seldom mistook a hawk for a hand-saw.

They also razzed each other. While Spike and I were on Four, they had brought in a charming Episcopalian rector who had tried to emulate Saint Francis by undressing in his pulpit. He had sat at table at

Spike's left, and Spike had afterward found a gener-
ous helping of mashed potatoes and gravy in his
pocket.

Of course, we had hundreds of privately shared
stock jokes, which we wore thin, as groups do in
boarding schools and boarding houses. A favorite was
the squirrels. They were all over the place, on the
lawns, in the trees, tame and familiar as in Central
Park. But that wasn't all. Our main buildings were
covered with ivy, and the ivy was filled with them.
They scurried up and down, along the eaves and roofs,
perched on second and third floor windowsills, peeking
in at us with their glittering eyes through bars and
screens. We rang endless changes on the theme of
squirrels at the nut college. Mostly it was cheap
humor, but sometimes it twisted toward distorted fan-
tasy of the Edgar Allan Poe sort. Our humor sometimes got out of hand. The bars and screens were not
to imprison but protect us. We were a vast granary
and the squirrels were swarming on our walls like rats.
But generally the twists we gave the squirrel theme
were less macabre if only middling funny. One day on
the lawn when little Professor Burke was following
some timid ones to feed them breadcrumbs, Hauser
shouted:

"Come here, everybody, and see this. If a squirrel chases a nut, it's not news. But when a nut pursues a squirrel, I ask you."

Yet our dear doctors—for our sakes—strove valiantly to inculcate among us the use of a more seemly vocabulary with reference to the institution and ourselves. Mental, mental, mental! "Mental hygiene! Mental cases! Mental hospital! Mental therapy!" Mental, mental, who's got the mental? Maybe the doctors had.

"Please do not think of yourself as an 'inmate' here," pleads able Pot-Belly, as kindly, competent, protective and well-wishing as ever man could be. "It would hurt *our* feelings, you know, if you thought of *us* as 'keepers.' "

It might modify outside opinion, soothe our families, soft-soap the sentimental, but to us who were locked up on the inside—and generally liking it, mind you—our usual answer was "Nuts!"

I should say that with the advent of May and June, outdoors in the park, the majority of us had as good a time, enjoyed ourselves as much, had "as much fun" literally, as any big crowd of eccentric, heterogeneous but congenial convalescents in the park of a war hospital or sanitarium in Carlsbad, Aix-les-Bains or California. I believe this was true of our Tarzans and

Julius Caesars from the back halls as much as for those
of us who were never violent and had no fixed delusions.

But there was very definitely one group of whom
this was tragically untrue. The sights, scenes and life
inside an insane asylum—while containing a larger
element perhaps of cheerfulness and good humor than
the outside public may imagine—are sometimes som-
ber, cruel in a way which has no connection with
human brutal guardians or chains, heartbreakingly
pathetic.

Spike, who had been through the mill, often said I
saw nothing, knew nothing. And once in Spike's company a friend of his named Clark, who had been in the
place two years, on all of the back halls at one time or
another, now slowly cured in mind and body, nearly
ready to go home and begin his life anew, said:

"Spike is right, you know. You don't know anything.
You have never seen anything. You have never been
through anything of course—but you have never seen
anything either."

"Well, what is it I don't know? Tell me. What is
it you fellows mean when you say to us who have only
been on the front halls, 'You guys don't know anything.'"

Clark said:

"Well, I don't know whether I could tell you. You see, we don't mean rough stuff. There aren't any hidden padded cells, dungeons or torture chambers. I don't mean fights with the attendants, smashed furniture—though I've seen furniture smashed, and faces too. It may surprise you when I say you needn't waste much sympathy on any violent case. So long as a man howls and screams, tries to break out, tries to kill the attendants, you needn't waste much sympathy on him. I went through that stage myself, among other stages, and I can remember some of it. I was excited, in rages. Well, a man who is excited, in a violent rage, isn't awfully unhappy, even when he's crazy. Not even if he hurts himself or gets hurt. He's mad as hell and don't care. When Charlie Logan howls like a wolf, the doleful noise might break your heart, but Charlie is partly enjoying it. He is enjoying howling, enjoying his suffering. I should say you needn't sympathize too much, even, with the patient who tries to commit suicide. He's still interested in something. He still wants something. He wants to die. He wants a wrong thing, but he wants it. You could hear, or see, or experience everything that goes on among such cases, and you still wouldn't know anything."

"Well, what in the devil do you and Spike mean?"

I said. "I sometimes think you're just a pair of old maids in a hospital bragging that nobody was ever quite as sick as you were."

We were sitting in a big double swing, on the lawn, near the paved walk which led up into the woods. The patients of Hall Three, some dozen of them, following their nurse, Miss Helmquist, were passing on one of their strolls.

Clark said in an undertone:

"There, that's what I mean, but you can't know what it means. That's the most awful thing that can happen to a human being. That's the deepest depth, the worst."

I looked at them now as they passed. I had seen them many times before, and never spoken to them, but knew some of their names vaguely. I wondered now whether I perhaps had an inkling, without understanding, what Clark did mean. We habitually took little active notice of this Hall Three "delegation" because it was the most quiet group of all, and had become, as we spent more and more hours outdoors, a permanent, familiar, part of the scene. But I remembered that I had first been stirred, disturbed more than a little, by the picture they made, and now, after what Spike and Clark had said, the silent procession which passed us slowly toward the woods gained a new, dark quality of mystery.

Ten mutes, ten ghosts, ten living dead men, shuffling single file, heads sunken on their breasts, passed silently into the shadows of the grove, led by a girl in white, pale, golden-haired, strayed from the pages of some horror-laden, German fairy-tale.

When they arrived at some rustic benches on the slope, the girl in white, I knew, would seat them scattered, singly or in twos, and read or knit for hours while her charges sat like dejected images or corpses, with mouths which occasionally mumbled but from which words never issued, eyes which stared but saw nothing, and ears—I had supposed—which heard no conscious sounds, for when I had first remarked them the first warm days of spring, one of my own attendants, or it may have been a fellow-patient, had said:

"They don't know whether they're outdoors or still back on their Hall. They're in such a fog that nothing matters to them. You could say anything you pleased to one of them, and he wouldn't bat an eyelid."

Yet Spike and Clark, who had once been for months in that living dead men's gallery, were telling me they suffered horribly.

That is, Clark was trying to tell me, but he said

that it was hard to remember. It is always similarly hard to remember, he said, precisely what intense physical agony is like after the pain is over. An impacted wisdom tooth or a thumb caught in a slammed automobile door. You remember it, he said, but not really.

He said:

"I can tell you it is a state of total, absolute despair, but how can I make you understand what it means? When a man attempts suicide, it means he cares about something. He cares whether he's alive or dead. He still wants something. He wants to be dead. He isn't in total despair. There's still something he can do about it, still a door of escape open. But real despair means there is no hope, no door, no escape. As a matter of fact, we never do try to commit suicide in that circle of hell, which is the lowest of all. It is as if we were already dead, rotting, yet still suffering. As if though we were dead, being eaten by worms, we still felt, *thought* and suffered.

"The awfulest part of it, of course, is that we still do think. We are not in a blank, dazed coma of suffering, as those men seemed to be who passed just now. It seems to be part of the disease that we must hide it. You see, we know we are crazy, we know we are mentally sick as can be, so we must never scream, complain, laugh or smile. To smile would be raving madness. Anything we might say would be the raving of a maniac, so we say nothing. But we think, continually, disjointedly. I can remember something of that for you—things I used to think—but I suppose each individual has different furniture and pictures in his own private chamber of horrors, and I doubt very much whether the thoughts will appear as anything but stupid and commonplace worries, certainly not fantastic or dramatic. Say, here's an angle that is quite interesting to me—the angle that the things you think in that state are intrinsically downright dull rather than nightmarish or fantastic. Let's see. I think it may surprise you:

"I sit. I am not sleepy. I can't read, write, play games, converse or engage in any occupation. I underestimate my financial resources; I am ruined, irrevocably ruined; things will always get worse from now on instead of ever better; my family will starve and I will become a state charge; I will have inmates like myself as associates; I will be abused and ill-treated; I will have a slow, long-dragging shameful end. My brain and will are diseased, but I have some horrible incurable physical disease too. The doctors know it, but try to keep it secret from me. No, it is I who am keeping it a secret from the doctors. Every time one of them asks me a question, no matter how trivial, or looks at my teeth, or touches me, I am in danger of revealing it. Whatever I answer will be seen through, so I must not answer at all. I must never complain of a headache or of being constipated when someone smiles and asks how I am; I must hide everything. My state is hopeless. And I myself am to blame for it. I convict myself, and there is no hope. I have only loathing and contempt for myself. I have no excuse for myself, not even any pity. I accuse myself continually, and find myself always guilty."

Clark finished this sample soliloquy, and looked at Spike for confirmation. Spike said:

"Naw, that's all rot. You've forgotten. You make it up, all except the part about self-accusation. You try to make it sound interesting. It was ten times blacker and duller. I know mine was. I couldn't even smoke. If it had been like you say—even allowing that my set of worries was worse than yours—I'd have been smoking all the time. Had plenty of cigarettes. I always smoke a lot when I worry. I couldn't smoke at all."

They argued, like a couple of bragging old maids

on the piazza of a convalescent home, about what the worst suffering had been and which one had suffered the most. The only thing they agreed on was that it was a million times worse than being "haywire," which was the local slang for hallucinated and violent.

"The guy," said Spike, "who tries to tear trees up by their roots, or thinks he's Julius Caesar or a chicken—even a chicken in a pot or about to have its head whacked off—is in a cheerful and grand state, compared to those birds up there who just sit."

We were interrupted by Charlie Logan, our pet paranoiac, the most popular patient in the whole institution, who had come over to bum a cigarette from Spike, and said cheerfully, as he was getting a light from Miss Pine:

"Darling, if I weren't already as crazy as a hoot-owl, I'd certainly go crazy about you."

XIII

WE USED to have long and complicated arguments, now that we were all out-doors, about Charlie Logan—why we all liked him so much, why all the attendants and doctors too always brightened up at the sight of Charlie. Visitors likewise, though at first inclined to be afraid of him, ended generally by becoming as fond of him as we were.

It was not in any sense that Charlie was a comical "nut" of the vaudeville type or a pet "village idiot." He had an average sense of humor and occasionally made fairly amusing wisecracks with the female nurses, but was never silly or ludicrous. He was not a type to arouse pity, nor did he ever seek it. He sat often alone, plucking daisies or loafing, under a tree on the hillside, and reminded me somehow of a lonesome cowboy, a youngish cowboy from down toward the Rio Grande or Mexico. He was small, with a small, round head, covered with short, smooth, black hair which grew as thick as a seal's fur, and level eyes of the same inky black set in a smooth, square-jawed, virile face. He looked—I don't know why—as if he might have been born in a covered wagon and survived an Indian massacre. As a matter of fact, he was from Brooklyn, and had worked in a clothing store. A reason why he made me think of the wild West may have been that on moonlight nights and when the weather changed he howled like a wolf or a coyote, back there somewhere on Hall Eight or Nine, and the sound would sometimes come to us through open windows. It was not unmusical. It had a certain quality of the open ranges. We would listen critically, and say, "That's Charlie. He's doing well tonight." Another reason I had wrongly felt him western may have been that he resembled an actor whose name I have forgotten, who played the rôle of the killer years ago in Owen Wister's *Virginian*.

The first time I had ever seen Charlie was in the gymnasium basement, in the winter, where the wild ones were permitted to prowl under Timothy's chaperonage when the rest of us weren't using the bowling alleys. He was marching up and down the long aisle beside the alleys, swearing loudly at himself in a sort of cadence which kept rhythm with the tramping feet, and took no notice of me as I passed. Timothy said affectionately:

"That's Charlie Logan. He's getting some of it out of his system. You must talk with him some day. He's a strange one."

Some weeks later, in January I think, I happened to be standing facing him while we were being checked out, over in the occupation lobby. This time he saw me for the first time, I imagine—stared a frank, level stare, and spoke in a frank, level, casual voice, a sort of intimate monotone, as if we had known each other intimately and shared our secrets for twenty years:

"How long have *you* been in here? What are you doing in this place? Are you married? Did your wife have you committed? Think you'll ever get out? What's the matter with you? What did you do for a living? How much money have you got?"

Now, why I didn't turn away from the madman, avoiding him, or why I didn't tell him it was none of his damned business, even though he was crazy, involves the same problem, I suppose, of why everybody in the place brightened up at the sight of him, or merely when his name was mentioned. I certainly had no feeling of "humoring" him, no sense of tolerating him as one might a child or savage, no aggressive idea

either of out-matching him in candor. And at least one
of his questions would have annoyed me, coming from
an own brother. So I did not know then, and do not
know now, why I found myself replying in almost his
own casual, familiar tone, that I'd been in since early
December; that I was in for alcoholism, drunkenness;
that I had been married but was now divorced and
had not yet married another wife; that I had committed myself with the help of friends; that I hoped to
get out eventually, but maybe only after a year or
so; that I wrote for a living; and (a detail which not
even my lawyer knew) that I had approximately such-
and-such a sum left in my bank balance and such-and-
such negotiable stock.

We were now brothers, or at least Charlie felt we
were. I hope he was right. We walked together when
we were checked out of occupation and marched over
to the gymnasium. I let the volley ball slide that
morning, and talked with Charlie. Before we finished,
he had imparted astoundingly intimate details of his
own life and plight, and I had done the same. He was
more prying and candid, more purified of pride,
hypocrisy and shame, than an honest man's own con-
science. I hope I am honest and without much pride,
but in answering his questions, I learned more about

myself than I might have been willing to admit in a silent wrestling match with my own ego.

I gathered, subsequently, that this was Charlie's normal, unconscious—or perhaps it would be better to call it abnormal—attitude, approach, "technique," toward all his fellow human beings. He would ask people, fellow-patients, doctors, attendants, visitors, *any-thing*—sometimes questions saintly in their searchings, more rarely obscene—taking for granted that he would receive answers, and willing at all times to reciprocate with equal candor. A consequence was that he always knew everything about everything and everybody in the institution, yet he was neither spy, sneak, nor gossip. He arrived at his facts openly and proclaimed them as openly, without twittering, huddling or malice. I sometimes thought that he would inevitably have been canonized if he'd been shut up in an eleventh century monastery instead of a twentieth century mental hospital.

Pot-Belly told it on himself one day that Charlie had pricked the bubble of one of his own dearest self-delusions, held since he had quit the German universities. And frequently, as, for instance, when somebody asked Dirk if Miss Blythe had ever been married, or somebody else asked if Sally Pine were pure-blood

American, the answer would be, matter-of-fact and unhumorous:

"You'd better ask Charlie Logan. He'll tell you if he wants to."

A climax, which filled us with a certain awe rather than shocks or snickers, came one afternoon outdoors, when he asked that most lovable and friendly, if somewhat imposing, society matron, Mrs. Frainer, whether she had had an orgasm when her son, there seated disconsolately like a pigeon on the grass, had been conceived.

She had turned brick-red, but smiled sadly and said:

"No, Charlie, I did not. But I love my son, and his father."

"Surely," said Charlie with sympathetic deference —and, after a pause, ". . . I thought so . . . but you can't blame him."

I hope I am giving you a picture of Charlie Logan, but I realize, of course, that I am not explaining him, and am probably not explaining, either, why everybody held him in affection. Charlie was "possessed," he was a crazy man, but apparently possessed by gnomes or angels rather than by demons. I have been presenting him in high-lights. He wasn't always so interesting; he sometimes fell into rages, and oftentimes sat morosely by himself, a lonesome cowboy. His curiosities, sometimes inspired and searching, were as frequently monkey-like and trivial. The mystery was that in whichever category they fell, no one seemed ever to resent them. The first time he ever saw Marjorie, he said, when I had introduced them:

"How'd you get that scar on your forehead? Did he give it to you? Do you think he'll ever be cured? Is that bracelet real?"

Marjorie is a reserved and easily embarrassed person, generally dumb when she meets people for the first time. I listened in considerable surprise—despite previous knowledge of Charlie's disarming directness —while she told him all about the scar, how many stitches had been taken in it, how long the doctor had said he thought it would take to fade, how Man Ray had helped us design the bracelet in Paris, and how the little silversmith who lived way over by the Buttes Chaumont had made three trips by bus across to Montparnasse with soft zinc models and his satchelful of Liliputian anvils and hammers, before he got it to fit just right.

Sane friends, intimate, sane acquaintances, had more than once asked her about the bracelet which was of unusual design, but her replies were usually the customary, dumb, polite banalities.

She was frequently afraid of waiters, clerks, switch-

board operators, haughty saleswomen, people at teas
and literary cocktail parties, her own publisher—or
seemed to be—but she wasn't afraid of Charlie,
though she knew, as everybody did, that Charlie was
a crazy man who howled like a wolf and at intervals
"took on" the huskies.

Charlie seemed to have a code about uncorking his
wild stuff, though they hadn't yet been able to break
him from uncorking it. During the whole two years he
had been there, the attendants told me, he had never
attacked a fellow-patient, visitor, or doctor, yet every
so often he would go to the mat with the whitecoats,
or with one, or several, of Tim's gymnasium assistants.
Timothy had a theory, which I doubt whether the
psychiatrists would have subscribed to, that these
rampages of Charlie's were good for him. "Charlie,"
he would nod approvingly, while Charlie was trying
to bite, gouge, kick, choke, slug, commit various forms
of mayhem on several agile attendants who would be
trying, like Frank Buck, to net him alive, unscratched,
"is getting some of it out of his system again."

I asked Charlie once why he never attacked anybody but the huskies, and he said:

"That's what they get paid for. I have to help them
earn their money."

Of course there were other wild men—"disturbed patients" was the anodyne official phrase—who could not be similarly trusted. These too were brought out in the sunshine, brought to the gymnasium on rainy days, kept in the park for long hours, but always accompanied by watchful attendants, continually on their toes, trained to think fast and act faster in any crisis. Eternal vigilance on the part of the attendants was the price of liberty and sunshine for patients who less than a generation ago would have been locked in padded cells.

This whole phase of modern psychiatric therapy, it seemed to me, was legitimate and successful . . . if costly. I am not using costly as a weasel-word or metaphor. I do not mean that it was costly in terms of gouged eyes or broken bones. I mean that this modern system is obviously more expensive to the institution in terms of actual money. It requires more and better attendants. They didn't have to pay salaries to straitjackets or work handcuffs in eight-hour shifts. And you, on the outside, need have no misgivings that if you ever visit such a park—as a visitor—your life, limbs or dignity will incur any danger. A proof that the institution was right in releasing such patients, untrammeled, into open air and sunshine, and even permitting certain "maniacs" like Charlie Logan to mingle with us and with visitors, lies in the fact that over the long decade this system has been in operation, there is no single case on record in which a violent patient has harmed another patient or a visitor. Rare suicides do still occur, despite incessant vigilance, but injury inflicted by patients on each other never.

A large class of these modernized mental hospitals is now formally committed to the absolute and literal abolition of all cells, muffs, hobbles, straps, restraining apparatus, likewise to all forms of isolated confinement. The system they have substituted for physical restraint is fantastic, and leads occasionally to frantic distress on the part of the staff responsible for our safety, as during a twenty-four hours last winter when an old-fashioned razor disappeared mysteriously from the locked steel drawer in the barber-shop. As Spike said, "It looked for a while as if all the doctors would go crazy." They had not merely searched all our persons, rooms and belongings, but had begun to look in hollow trees and were tearing up the carpets, when Eddie, the barber, recalled he had sent several razors to be honed, and that while the return-slips checked up, he couldn't swear the actual razors had.

By fantastic, I mean simply that I never got over the strangeness of being invited to play tennis and croquet, or stroll picking dogwood blossoms with paranoiacs, schizophrenics, and dementia praecox cases who less than twenty years ago would have been fed through the bars.

In the comparatively short seven months I stayed there, I saw some of them come out of it, as demon-ridden men came out of it in the miracles by Galilee. My hat is off to the psychiatrists, even to Dr. Quigley. It was a place of miracles as well as sanctuary. It impressed me so deeply that I remember being surprised that there seemed to be one class of miracle they couldn't perform. I don't think they could ever change the essential nature of the patients. I am sure that Charlie Logan was lovable before he ever went crazy and still will be if he ever gets well. A likeable person remains likeable even in insanity, and a crazy Armenian is still an Armenian when he walks out cured. I remember how much this surprised me. I had confidently imagined he would be transformed into a Bavarian. It distressed me that certain mean, irritable crazy men on the back halls were still mean and irritable when they moved, cured, to the villas. It made me know I would always be a neurasthenic man, a frequently unhappy man, afraid of life, whether they cured me of being a drunken man or not.

XIV

TOWARD the end of May, leading this new life outdoors, becoming now an inmate, as it were, of the whole big institution, it began occurring to me—for the first time—that when I got out of the place I would surely write something about it. I hope that wasn't the whole reason why I began preferring the company of Charlie Logan and the wild men from the "back halls" to that of my own convalescent playmates on the front halls and in the villas. I don't believe it was the whole reason. Wanting honestly to be as honest as I can, I feel sure it wouldn't be true to say that I sought their friendship and confidence merely for sensational copy. All my life I have preferred the company of Dostoevsky, Herman Melville, Poe, Rimbaud, Verlaine, to that of Tennyson, Oliver Wendell Holmes, and Milton. So that I cannot feel I was insincere in preferring Charlie and his crew.

Be that as it may, I will confess to an unadulterated, shameless, catlike curiosity to know what life was like *inside* those back halls from which Charlie and his crew emerged each day to play with the rest of us in the park.

Everybody knows now what the padded cells, strong rooms, cages, chains and camisoles were like in places where "raving maniacs" were habitually confined less than a generation ago, and knows that they have been cleaned up, ameliorated since Victorian days, but I for one had been completely ignorant of what this part of the interior of a modernized asylum might be like, and I imagine that most of the outside public has only the vaguest idea of precisely how these bedlams have been reformed.

Prompted then both by plain curiosity and by what I hope may pass as honest interest too, I began asking the attendants, patients, nurses, huskies, Charlie, Phillip Reed (whom I have not yet properly introduced to you) to tell me everything they could, or would, about what "went on" in the back halls where Charlie howled like a wolf on moonlight nights and epic battles were frequently staged with singularly few casualties or scratches.

The fact that I had changed from convalescent drunkard to inquiring reporter was promptly written down on my chart, caused Papa Duval some slight distress and was duly noted at staff conference, I'm told, but it aroused no misgivings or antagonism whatever on the part of the staff, the doctors, the directors, not even on the part of Dr. Quigley. They didn't care, for the best of all reasons. They had long since let in the sunlight. They had nothing to cover up or hide, no Count of Monte Cristo, no heirs or heiresses in chains, no skeletons in closets. Soon nurses, superintendents, fellow-patients, doctors, began asking just what I might care to know and volunteering information. I preferred to get most of it from the hired huskies and the Charlie Logans, checking them back and forward on each other, often provoking and hearing curious arguments. And I managed, of course, before leaving the place, to visit the back halls and see with my own eyes.

The so-called "strong room" which has replaced the once-classic, literal "padded cell," is something no theatrical producer or fiction writer could possibly have concocted from imagination unless he had actually seen one. It is a medium-sized, squarish room, with cream-colored, smooth, hard-finished walls and a dark-brown linoleum floor, absolutely bare, void as interstellar space, except for a postless bed fastened immovable in the exact center of the floor, covered with

heavy, smooth rubber bedspread and pillow, the same
color as the floor. At first, it looked as if there was
nothing more to see—nothing that even Sherlock
Holmes with his magnifying glass could have discovered, but the doctor who was showing me the place
pointed with pride to the door-hinges. They were
rounded at their tops, stream-line, "sliding off," as he
aptly put it. I had never thought of this, but with a
bit of cord, a pair of shoestrings or a belt, you can
hang yourself from an ordinary door-hinge. From one
of these, on the contrary, you couldn't have hung a
mouse. And the lock of the knobless door, so help me,
instead of being metal, was made of flexible rubber!
My, were the doctors proud of that! I mentioned Rube
Goldberg, but they assured me they had invented it
themselves. When the rubber latch was in place, the
door could stand closed without banging, but neither
by intent nor accident could the door ever be really
locked, from either side, nor could it jam.

If the doors were weirdly scientific thus, the windows went to an opposite extreme. They were triple—
that is, each window had three "layers" in its ten-inch
thick box frame. On the extreme outside were camouflaged steel bars; next, for the middle layer, were ordinary window sashes which could be raised and lowered

at will by the attendants, regulating ventilation and temperature; the third window, the inside one, the only one the patient could get his hands or fists on, was partly shatter-proof plate glass and partly open steel-mesh grating.

But the first thing I should describe, I suppose, is the halls themselves, the stage-set, the routine. I'll take Hall Eight. A long corridor like a hotel corridor, linoleum-floored, bare-walled but with comfortable stuffed armchairs and sofas too heavy to be thrown about, widening out into a parlor furnished like a rather bare hotel lobby but with nothing that can be picked up or torn off the wall and used as a rough-house weapon. A series of bedrooms with doors always wide open give on the public corridor. All windows are grill-barred, camouflage-barred, as I have described. They let in all the sunlight but prevent patients from smashing the glass for amusement. Bedrooms are equipped with bed, wardrobe-bureau, unbreakable mirror screwed to wall, and a chair. The attendants keep the keys to wardrobe-bureaus and all clothes are locked up at night, belts, suspenders, things like that of course, but all ordinary clothes too, for it is not impossible for a man to strangle himself with a shirt-sleeve.

Patients eat, those who can be persuaded, in a common dining room, with knives, forks and everything,
but with hawk-eyed attendants eternally alert. They
are never permitted anything with a point or cutting
edge except under the actual eyes of the attendants.
But from morning to night, indeed at all hours of the
day and night, locked within the large confines of the
hall or out in the park, they are completely at liberty
within those limits, at all times free of any mechanical
or physical restraint, free, consequently, to sit in their
own rooms or wander about mingling with their playmates, free to start private wars, incipient riots, mas-
sacres, to try to take the place to pieces or turn it inside out at any time the impulse strikes them. The
answer obviously is a three-shift crew of hand-picked,
alert whitecoats, half of them graduate male nurses
and all of them experts in plain and fancy wrestling.
The game has rules, and the attendants take pride in
it. The patient has all the advantage of being permitted and expected to gouge, slug, kick, and hit below
the belt, while the whitecoats must net him unscathed,
unscratched, unbruised, and as nearly unhurt as is
humanly possible. There is an ironclad rule that they
can never stop a patient with their fists, no matter
what the provocation. They must let him come and

take him as Doctor Ditmars takes a sick tiger. The whitecoats are permitted, necessarily, to "gang" the tiger and it sometimes takes three or four whitecoats to surround and net him. They are so good at it, that patients soon get discouraged, and the result is, I am told by veteran attendants who once worked in other institutions with straitjackets, padded cells and handcuffs, that there is surprisingly little violence— much less indeed than there used to be when patients were tied up or locked like animals in solitary confinement. Patients now were injured by manhandling almost never, though from time to time gorgeous battles were staged from which some hapless whitecoat might emerge looking as if he'd been in a football game with the marines, and be kidded for a week by fellow attendants and patients alike because of a black eye, cracked shin or bitten hand done up in bandages. I'm not wanting to paint this as perfect or the whitecoats as archangels. They have on occasion lost their tempers. Patients have been socked on the jaw and attendants fired for it, but compared with the way these shows once were run, it seems to me the new way is something modern mental hospitals can shout about. They still, as a matter of fact, seem to have a hangover reluctance from the old straitjacket days of saying much about it themselves except in technical journals which the general public never reads, but it seems to me that they can justly be proud of it and that I can consequently hope they won't be annoyed by my telling it.

"Just the same, Spike, what happens when a patient not only goes haywire, but stays haywire . . . when a fellow runs amuck, I mean . . . and keeps on trying to smash everybody and everything? What do they do with him after he's netted, so to speak?"

"Well, if it's just a prolonged hysterical or nervous crisis, you know already what they do. You had a taste of it yourself. Prolonged baths and the pack. But they never keep a guy in the pack for long. If he stays on a permanent rampage they throw him in the room at the end of the hall. You saw it yourself, I guess. It's a room with nothing but a clamped-down bed in it and a door that always stays wide open. It isn't padded or anything, it's just a big room with the door always wide open like I've told you. We called it the "strong room" but that was a misnomer because it's wide open. When a guy is in there, two attendants simply sit at the open door, playing cards or reading detective stories, and when he tries to come out they throw him back. They attend to his wants, and go in if he starts banging his head against the wall, or mistakes the middle of the room for a latrine, but their main job is just to sit there and throw him back. But look here, if we keep telling you all this stuff, you'll end by writing stuff that isn't true at all. You can believe it or not, but *nine-tenths of the time life is as quiet, as peaceful, as well-ordered on those back halls as it is on the front halls or in the villas. If you think, from the high-lights we give you, that it's always in a turmoil back there, you won't know what it's like at all. You might be locked in one of them yourself for a week and never know you weren't in the corridor of an ordinary hospital.*"

We were talking in a swing, beneath the trees, near one of the drinking fountains. Phillip Reed had rambled over, and said with a pink, noisy chortle:

"Not always, Spike! Remember the snapping turtle? Remember our dear Dr. Remsen?"

Spike remembered—and they told me about Dr. Remsen. Phillip told me the most of it, Spike merely confirming. I got subsequent confirmation of its essential details later from the attendants, but first of all it will be necessary to explain Phillip. Phillip was special, not typical. He was a handsome youth who had been born with a golden spoon in his mouth and a transplanted British ancestry which had known since the time of George II how to handle gold spoons naturally. Precocious, artistically inclined and nervous, he had been educated by a string of the best private tutors England and New England could provide, and had been taken by his family on more than one occasion to the continent. But Phillip's father had been killed in the war, and Phillip's mother, always neurasthenic, had to be put away in a place not very dissimilar to the place we were now in. When Phillip's trustees and the family lawyers and doctors consulted with Phillip about Phillip's future, it developed that Phillip himself was a dementia praecox case, and with the hope of having him cured rather than merely to get rid of him, they had sent him here. Phillip knew all about it, knew that he was a dementia praecox case, knew that this was the best place for him to be, and made the best of it. I have said that he was not typical. He was one of the most brilliant, if crack-brained, youths I have ever met, and had apparently read everything culturally readable from the ancient Greeks to the modern Ulysses. His flashings would have been almost impossible to reproduce at second hand, and after he had told us the tale of the snapping turtle, I asked him if he would some day write it down for me.

He had a typewriter in his room. They wouldn't let him have a pencil, but he couldn't hurt himself with a typewriter. He subsequently wrote it for me and I am going to reproduce it as he wrote it, and I am not sure that it isn't, perhaps, of superior interest to anything I've written myself. It will have this double revealing quality, at any rate, of depicting an inside episode in a place of this sort as seen through the eyes of an actually "disturbed" inmate. I have not edited it or attempted to change sentence-construction or punctuation. Except for the elimination of certain exuberant, unprintable obscenity which I have been forced to delete, it stands here exactly as he wrote it. As to the essential veracity of the episode-series and the aptness of the caricature he has drawn of his fellow-patient, I have ample confirmation from Spike and others.[1]

Here is Phillip's piece:

"He was one of the funniest people I will ever meet, one dr andrew k remsen, a patient with me on

---

[1] AUTHOR'S NOTE: "Dr. Storm," who generously read and approved my manuscript as a whole, disagrees about this material of "Phillip's." He says, *"It certainly is not the account concerning one patient but probably a composite picture of several. I cannot help but think your book would be better without it."* I think it belongs in the text, however, as a *subjectively* true picture of a disturbed hall as seen through the eyes of a *disturbed* patient.

hall five, but to properly decode this epic you must realize that I am gifted or cursed with a very immature sense of humor which you will see only too well as this narrative continues.

"I shall first describe our subject. Our subject is short, not more than five-foot six in height, his face has a rugged cast, resembling, with its super-strong aquiline nose and rather square massive head, nothing so much as a snapping turtle, a small, pesky, stocky, energetic snapping turtle in the heyday of his meanness and general cussedness. The effect is furthered to almost unbelievable realism by his gait. Apparently he had more or less lost the control of certain of his knee flexors beyond a point in extension of about one hundred and seventy degrees. These joints were also hyperextensive. This combination gave the effect of a turtle walking on its hind flippers . . . somewhat the same as the classical illustration of the walrus with the carpenter . . . as the knee-joints are invariably carried into extreme hyper-extension while with each step the toes point outward!! Among his peculiar qualities are:—he has delusions of persecution insomuch as he thinks that all the nurses and attendants are ruffians out to get him; he has a distinctly and violently split personality insofar as he considers himself two different people, one of whom is 'that dirty old man, dr. remsen, who is always spitting at me,' and the other some ideally brutal and heroic individual who gives that 'dirty old man' some terrible beatings up. These beatings are of so strenuous a nature that I have seen the old boy knock himself coldernafrosenfishesarsole, and he's always in possession of either a lovely lump on the jaw or a marvellous shiner —all, mind you, self inflicted.

"Whenever one clacked the tip of one's tongue against the roof of one's mouth or made that hoarse sound which is produced by the forced passage of air between the tongue and the palate . . . not a bronx cheer . . . he would go through the most astounding gyrations and either end up by spitting at you with various imprecations or swatting himself on the jaw. One of my favorite occupations was to make one or the other of these noises while seated on a piano stool. He would then begin by touching his left elbow with his right-hand fingertips, then the point of his jaw technically known as the button. His next step was to arise from his accustomed position on the couch . . . I do not believe he ever sat anywhere else during his long residence on hall five! . . . and proceed to go through a set of the most astonishing movements imaginable.

"With a slow, grave waltzing motion . . . perfect three-quarter time! . . . he would start turning about in a circle accompanied with churning motions of the arms and legs and squealing sounds comparable only to the sounds made by a vicious mare having the stud put to her. Before going further with this recontation of my most beloved nut, I think I had better say more about the quality of these sounds he makes when under duress, or should I say I'll interrupt this narrative—"

Here there is a break in the letter followed by some lines of incoherent reference to Phillip's own suffering. Then it re-begins:

"It is twentyfour hours since I wrote the last lines and today has been a sort of grisly nightmare for me, but that, god, I have kept concealed fairly well. It has been a sort of pursuit, flying from it, with it always at my side. If days to follow are like this one and nights like last night, I hope to heaven I become catatonic or something and insensible to psychic pain! I think that despite all this hellblackness I shall try to give you some more now about the classic andrew remsen though I do not feel so very funny right now.

"I believe I had got to the point where I was describing the walk and certain amusing actions of the

critter when the abyss opened and took all the haw-
haw out of me, but I seem to have myself more or less
under control again. As I before related, this strange
beast's actions included selfswatting to the point of
raising shiners and knocking himself stiff as a board.
Have I already told you that he had two and sometimes three totally different personalities? The most
offensive was 'that dirty old man, dr. remsen, who is
always spitting at me,' while the other one most in
evidence was the big ideal bully, 'joe brewer,' to whom
he always ascribed, when asked, any lesions, bruises or
other disfigurations of his own turtlesque physiognomy. He sometimes railed back at the brutal mr
brewer when he was socking himself with extra energy,
and accused the doughty brewer of ringing in helpers,
Hawaians, thugs of various sorts, and an offensive
gang from Kansas City. These gangfights with himself
would sometimes delay his retiring, and when the
night men came on the fun really started. When they
tried to persuade him to go to bed and sleep, he would
say, 'ha, night watchman, you don't like the noise,' and
then take to bellowing at the very peak of his voice,
'Moidah! Moidah! Help! Help! Help! Help!,' with
absolutely no expression of any emotion whatsoever in
his turtlelike, metallic voice. Sometimes it rose to a

highpitched, grating screech, until, if the night man were a particularly patient one and merely stood there through it, remsen would become silent, start spitting at him, and when that failed shut up like a clam and went quietly to bed.

"But if the nightman had the foolhardy courage to go so far as to help him undress..... ! ! ! ! ! ! ! - - - - boyoboyoboyoboyoboy! Howls the like of which have seldom been heard outside a monkeyhouse first split the cringeing air, arms, hands, feet, bedclothes, legs and furniture began to fly, with such profanity which blazed and corruscated from wall to wall that we listened in awestruck wonderment that turtlish rancour could assume these cosmic proportions—yet all delivered in his toneless, absolutely nevertobeduplicated, metallic voice.

"One night, I remember, last March, Pete Jennings was night charge on our hall, and decided that remsen was going to bed. When Pete decides a thing it is usually accomplished, and so at half past nine he walked into the old boy's room. First the usual hullaballoo bust loose while the turtle yelled for help eight or nine times, and then he began to swear and hit himself.

" 'Aha! You goddammed redheaded soviet nigger

(selfswattbam!) thought you'd sneak in through the window with your shoes off (selfswattbam!) but everybody knows your name you blinking son of a bastard-bitch, and how do you like that!'

"Punching and pummelling himself, he began to pant at the top of his voice as if he had been engaged in a mortal struggle with untold odds against him, and finally ended by panting out in the most ludicrously labored manner, 'So? You haven't had enough? You want some more!' Bam! Bam! Bam! Bam!..... 'ooooooohhh! stop! stop! I've had enough!' More labored panting, a few more desultory swipes at himself and all was finally calm for the rest of the night.

"This was what usually happened, but here is a different turtle tale. A young male nurse named Jack in his probationer days was working on our hall. Lilandrew for some unknown reason had dirtied his pants, and the young neophyte was detailed to see to it that the old beezark changed his clothes. He went down to the old laddy-buck's room and kindly suggested to him that he change his clothes. Andrew looked at him with an appearance of utter disdain, but slowly took off his coat as we crowded looking in the door. Having performed this operation he sat himself down in his chair and looked out of the window. Jack asked him presently to go on changing. He got up slowly, gave Jack another look of reproachful hostility, removed one shoe, then sat down again and looked out of the window some more. The neophyte, with the patience of a Christ, gently urged him to continue his disrobing. Finally andrew rose again with muttered blasphemy, picked up his hairbrush wherewith he right lustily batted himself on the right ear, and then sat down again. After more urging, he got himself up again wearily with the look of a martyr, slowly removed his other shoe, picked up a newspaper, sat himself down again in his chair and began to read.

"The new nurse had now lost patience and said, 'It's your trousers you must take off, change. If you don't I'll get help and take them off you.'

"Andrew now rose with the look of one worn out almost to the point of fainting, a longsuffering look of benevolent hatred . . . yes, he could produce so paradoxical a look and never or ever again will there be another like him! . . . then fumblingly removed his belt and started. Slowly, unbuttoningly, funeral-pacingly he finally got out of his trousers and underwear, then gyrating sent them flying filthily into the new attendant's face yelling, 'There, ye niggerfaced apachee, ya will try to scalp me, will yuh?'

"Joy reigned and was remsen to suffer for it, have no supper? Outside the windows snowbrown windstorming white in whiteness dimwrapped, inside all sat eating, for day darkened. While windsang I with mouthful watched my eatmates gulp till he, (o song for songingjoysakes!) for it was no other . . . guess you not who? . . . ha, comes, see ladies and gentlemen, it walks, it looks, it is a snappingturtle! Now kindly note take noteness and observe this strange obfiddium avant your orbs—jawswollen from selfsocking repeatedlike and redface—you will observe naught else than the reincarnation of the one, the only and original daniel boon turtle, dr andrew remsen, (pronounced askewe). Gingerly he, inpouring, sluslupping, slupoogalling soup mid face pinchingeyeblinks menagerie squeelings. Then came the meatcourse! . . . . ! ! Einsnow look not arscanz on what will follow! grandcanon was verrimachen, kinchenjunga beweldwrinklehumped milesdepth of oceanlife lacyfish living, so whynotho whatisho to follow? . . . . .

"whitedressed tom mckee the soup bore off and waited we the meat to come then it arrived. First I then to the left the viands passed, cabbage and lamb and murphies on the plates amassed, one and another turning headthought food, never expecting to be expecting that which came.

"Tom gently down the plate placed where with turtlelook and turtlenoise he then refused the food. You've touched it with your fingers, you, you dirty heathen, you are not my waiter, you nazi man! Abdominable I calls it. hif yew but gnu ow coverhandedly he germbugged allcrawlingly ye'd faint for he's a germyfraid fellah. For he's a germyfraid fellaaaaahhh!, for he's a germyfraid fellaaaaah!, for he's a germyfraid fellaaaah, a septiphobiyak! Pardon my hypomania but nuts refused and, my little one, when a turtle refuses naught can naysay him yea though mckee in firm but gentle bade him eat or leave the room, but the turtle would a nixing nix so there he sat downstonily until they brought him other food which they did not. In Spasmodia, it is greatly feared, according to our correspondent, that a state of war may soon exist between members of the League of Superiorly Submersible Snappingturtles and the Whitecoat Guild. Relations have been for some time in an acutely strained condition. Alltimingly brindle snowbrown light pervades the dining room. Nowords come lomuttered rambling from crackpot crannies oozing dry thin slime of wombwanderings. At mealend all eats must mealend all quiet was apparent chairscrapings; eclecticus maximus; but still stillsittish sat the snappingturtle; no move in either eye or flipper to be seen, poised turtlewise above his wouldnottasted meal. Then and then only intentadvanced did tom mckee approach the fatal table while I schemedawdled food before did sit expectant, innardly gleegurgling, o scene of scenes!

"Dr remsen, we want to clear the table now so would you please leave the room and not hold up the service any longer? You flatfaced fingler, you are not my waiter! Pantrymaid, o pantrymaid! Please call a policeman and have this impostor arrested, he's annoying our party. Sorry dr remsen but I've got to take those dishes. Stoppress! War declared. Our correspondent in Spasmodia has informed us that hostilities commenced today with a barrage of beefstew. This offensive led by General Andrew Frederick Remsen Boonturtle for a short period of time confused the forces of the Whitecoats, covering their uniform front with vast areas of brownish deposit. Our correspondent goes on to relate that the forces of the Guild became enraged at this untoward use of lethal liquids and retaliated with a counterbarrage of glasswater which completely submerged the Snappingturtles who, welltrained in the art of complete submersion felt no inconvenience at the onslaught but emitted their battlecry, 'Hoydleoydlehoy!'

"The Intraturtlary Flying Foetuses gyrated rapidly

in large hellical spirals above the conflict while the sun was effaced by gigantic clouds of sulphurous smoke emitted by the profanejectors of the league. The terrapin was littered with dead and wounded, inextricably mingled with remnants of cauls, veils, placentae and sluffages scattered by the forces of the League for purpose of tripingentangling the Guild's combatants. Upon the entanglements of braided naval cords protecting the League's trenches innumerable Guild soldiers were expiring, the air made hideous by their tortured shrieks and groans. But Guild survivors were not idle. Into the conflict they hurled new phalanxes of ants, traderats and tumblebugs armed by the teeth with high forceps, syringes, knouts, pessaries and progenical prophylactics, allarmclocks and shovels. A contingent of praying mantises heavily armed with casehardened phallusses marched into the fray to the strains of Paul Whiteman and were annihilated by a squad of the League's fighting spermatazoa armed with whiskbrooms of familiar public hair when General Boonturtle and General Lawnorder came to an emilliatory understanding. General Boonturtle struck the fighting colors of the League with a heavy Joebrewerish selfjawhook on the button and peace once more reigned in Spasmodia.

"Oh bated snapping turtle, I have sweated blood and tears to do you justice, but I do you wrong. So fearfully and wonderfully wraught was he that wildest mad behavior went often flipperhand with old-world courtliness of pleasant little gentleman indeed. His pipings and squealings would capture your heart, and while his squalls and yells were sotoneless metallic, mechanic, yet they had in them a lovely quality of gammonish littleturtlesitfulness. He was an infinitely sweet little porcupine all over sticcles and quills that rose whenever one can near him or was friendly, and now to quote my master, in the name of the Former and the Latter and their Holocaust; Allmen."

Phillip's favorite books, of course, were *Rabelais*, *Wasteland*, and *Ulysses*. They are among my favorites too—I truly do believe *Ulysses* will be granite when most of our now current so-called literature is tinsel dust—and my inclusion of what Phillip wrote has been for no cheap, silly purpose of subjecting Joycian style to ridicule by reproducing a burlesque of it by a man shut up in an insane asylum. I have quoted Phillip, on the contrary, because I liked what he wrote, felt that it helped fill out the picture I am trying to paint in my own plain journalistic prose. I have been tempted to include at this point a whole small portrait gallery of Phillip's eccentric, deranged, hall-companions as seen through Phillip's own eccentric, deranged eyes. But it will be a more honest, though less colorful, piece of reporting, perhaps, if I simply outline instead a selected few of them as they appeared to me.

One who interested me particularly because I had read Strindberg's mad memoirs was an otherwise normal fellow who was continually plagued by hydraulic and electric pressure. There was nothing magic, occult or incredible about it, he explained to me. A man in the cellar was doing it, aided by a negress in the belfry, "and they had machines." They would put this pressure on various parts of his body, sometimes as he sat or walked with us in the park. "You fellows, help me take it off," he would sometimes suggest, but usually he was able himself to transfer it to the bench beside him, to a tree, or to the ground. He did this by what he called numerology, by rattling off logarithmic number-combinations which deflected the pressure. Otherwise he, or a given portion of his anatomy, would be crushed flat as a pancake.

Another was a sympathetic little Jewish carpenter who had killed his wife three times. He would tell you this as she sat beside him and held his hand, while he was telling it. She came faithfully every Wednesday and Friday. It was because he remembered, she said, how he, who had always been so tender, had fallen into rages at her after he became sick. He believed now that the asylum was going to discharge him and that if it did he would be convicted and electrocuted. So that he would often plead with attendants or doctors, "Keep me one more day, keep me until tomorrow."

One of the most angry and voluble patients, always on the defensive and always seeking an audience to air his woes, was a former Hollywood director, now forgotten, who had known Griffith and Lillian Gish way back when they were making *The Birth of a Nation.* His quarrel with fate, however, antedated Hollywood and the movies. He believed he was Pontius Pilate, and was always telling us about the dirty trick that had been played on him when he was Procurator of Judea. There had been the real Jesus, but there had also been a double, a man masquerading as Jesus who was a homosexual degenerate and criminal of the worst sort. So that he, Pontius Pilate, had convicted the real Jesus of all the things the false Jesus was guilty of. "Everybody was fooled as well as I," he would shout, "yet I got all the blame."

We had several reverse-English hunger strikers who compared symptoms and sometimes took the rest of us into their confidence. By reverse-English, I mean that none of them wished to starve or was imitating Gandhi. They wanted to eat. Oh, yes, but they were afraid to. One was afraid for the good old reason that the hospital attendants had been hired to poison him. Another explained to me that his stomach was too tiny, that it was a small sac, like an appendix. The one who had the worst time explained that everything he ate turned to cement. It seemed to me that they had simply given a mad, literal twist to common enough metaphorical ways of suffering chronic indigestion.

Concerning idiosyncrasy toward food, another patient confided to me a "secret" which may have some bearing on the curious psychotic food-taboos sometimes encountered among savages. This friend told me one day that he was in continual peril from the toast which was always served at breakfast.

"Poisoned?" I asked.

Oh, no, it wasn't poisoned. In fact, it wasn't the toast at all, he explained. It was *the toast's significance.*

"Eh?"

"Yes, and you can't realize how dangerous it is, because they frequently change the test. On one day, if I eat it, I confess I mean to set fire to the place. But on another day, if I refuse to eat it, it is proof that I am concealing a plan to set the place on fire."

A newcomer in May who delighted us all and enjoyed himself thoroughly as soon as he got used to the environment, was a fake-surly young bond salesman who had been to Yale and the best tailors. He was sore but cynical. He was in a bit of a fog, but knew he was in a bit of a fog, and knew that was why he had been sent here. He knew why we were there, too. We were a bunch of nuts, and though he was now in the same boat, he had a cocky contempt for all of us.

He soon became a member of Hauser's gang—they were our "professional comedians"—but only after they had shaken him down in a spelling bee. It began one night after supper, when Spike, who was Harvard, though you'd never guess it, and Hauser, who was Princeton, were kidding this Yale chap about his New Haven illiteracy—the usual stuff—when Hauser said:

"I'll bet you haven't even learned to spell!"

The newcomer accepted the challenge, and Hauser began, with pauses, of course, for the right or wrong answers:

"Spell touch, spell smell, smell spell, spell hear,

spell see. Spell Riders to the Sea. Spell Singh and Caruso."

"You're maudlin," interrupted the badgered victim at this point, who was manfully trying, but getting tangled.

"All right, spell maudlin. *Poifect!* Now spell Maudlin College. *Wrong.* Spell Singh again. Spell singe, spell singeing, spell Singeing Ervine, spell Gotterdammerung and Rheingold Weiss."

Finally Hauser said:

"Spell uranology. *Hey, wrong again, and you've got a dirty mind. It's planets! You're Yale all right.*"

Newcomers, new inmates, naturally interested us all immensely. One of the saddest tales of a newcomer in the hospital's modern history has been written down by my friend Phillip. It seems to be properly a part of the picture I am trying to fill in, since to be a true general picture it must have its dark shadows, but in this case I shall cut the script, edit it, and simply quote parts of Phillip. The facts, of course, are on independent record, or I shouldn't quote him in this instance at all.

"This," Phillip wrote, "concerned an aged judge, and should begin on Hall Four in which I spent some time after my first detention. I had been there only about three days when a 'new one' came in. He was a pathetic little fellow, weedy, stringy, horribly depressed. His eyes were glaucous behind a pair of gold-rimmed spectacles. He was totally bald save for a priest-like fringe at back, and his symptoms were distressing. He was for the most part quiet and mopey, scarcely answering when spoken to, or at best mumbling something unintelligible. At other times he was quite agitated, and it was during these periods that, after walking rapidly about and muttering to himself —a not uncommon symptom with us all—he would begin emitting what I can only describe as truly goat-like bleatings. Once he barricaded himself in his room, and later it transpired that he had an intermittent phobia about anybody entering a room in which he slept.

"When I was first moved from Hall Four I lost sight of the judge for several months, until on another hall I renewed acquaintance with him. He still occasionally became agitated and scurried about bleating, but somehow seemed better than he had been before. There were long spells during which he was rational, and we were all believing he would get well.

"There was a billiard room on the new hall where we were. One night we were all sitting round in a corner, some talking, others playing cards with the attendants, the judge and I together on a couch. We talked pleasantly, had our milk and played a game of pool together—the first he had played, he said, since entering the institution—and then after a few moments more of pleasant talk we all went to bed. I remember just before going to sleep thinking what a fine little man the judge was and what a shame it was that one so brilliant in the law and yet so profoundly human in his sympathies should have become demented. He had been dangerously ill, I said to myself, but how fine it was that he was now recovering.

"He occupied the room next to mine, and I was awakened at three o'clock one morning by his bleating. The bleating ceased and I went to sleep again with a feeling that here was a tortured soul recovering and soon to leave. Toward dawn I awakened again when the night watchman passed by my open door. At the next open bedroom door I heard him stop, gasp and hurry in. There was complete silence for a fraction of a minute, then he came quietly out of the room, locked the door behind him and hurried down to the broom-closet which housed the telephone. Five minutes later two of the doctors passed my door, unlocked the judge's and went in. They stayed a little while and went away, locking it again.

"At seven, the usual time we were awakened, Pop Elpham, the oldest attendant, came hurrying around to all our rooms with a cheerful smile to tell us that we were all going out for a little walk before breakfast, and so please to hurry with our dressing. It was a cold, drizzly gray March morning and we all wondered why we were being taken out before breakfast—a thing unparalleled in the hospital routine—but I felt that I knew and was sad in the knowledge.

"We tramped round and round in the circle for a quarter of an hour, slogging around in the slush and drizzle, and were then taken back to our hall. The little judge's room was open and empty."

I am including this dark shadow in my attempt to paint an honest picture of the institution toward which I am grateful for my own recovery, because I am sure that it can do no harm. The reason it can do no harm is that the "suicide statistics" for this and all similar American asylums in which mechanical restraint has been abolished, are amazingly, almost miraculously, low—lower than they ever were in the old days when suicidal patients were rigorously confined. It still hap-

pens. It is still the ever-present nightmare of doctors
and attendants, the reason for nine-tenths of the at-
first-silly-seeming regulations, but it happens so rarely,
and the record is so clean, that it would be useless
hypocrisy to pretend that it never happens. In a New
York Appellate Court decision handed down in Sep-
tember 1934, absolving a similarly conducted mental
hospital from both moral blame and legal liability in
the death by suicide of a demented patient, the Presid-
ing Justice wrote:

"I am unable to see in what was done for the deceased in the instant case anything other than what the
record shows to have been proper treatment. If we
could think of taking patients out for a walk as something quite impersonal, like the exercising of a horse,
the act well might be considered administrative; but,
accepting what the record shows, that nervous break-
downs with suicidal tendencies on the part of the victim are due to or bring about a loss of confidence and
the courage to face one's problems, and promote the
desire to find the easiest way out, through death, we
can understand that the restoration of confidence and
courage is the sine qua non to recovery and must of
necessity entail risks or leave the case hopeless. The

record does not show that restoration of confidence
and cure could be brought about if the patient believed
himself always under strict supervision. Perhaps nothing would be more depressing to him than a man at his
elbow every moment. The record makes it clear to my
mind that when a patient afflicted as was deceased is
convalescing, little by little more and more responsibility and liberty of action must be accorded him to
help him regain confidence in himself. The hospital
should not be held a guarantor. If it succeeds it means
life; if it fails the life remaining is without value. The
evidence makes all this clear. . . . No liability should
attend his death."

Phillip seems to have come into this more than I
had intended. Looking back I realize that if Charlie
Logan was for some peculiar reason—almost like ani-
mal chemistry—the most beloved member of our deranged, kaleidoscopic company, the flashingly demented and precocious Phillip was by far its most
brilliant. He had a complete contempt for my books,
of which he had read a couple—dismissed them as
trash—but liked to talk with me. He liked to talk
about himself and this was not boring for he had read

every available psychiatric book on his own malady and knew almost as much about it academically as the doctors. Next to talking about himself, the thing he liked most to talk about was modern literature. He spent half of his time reading, and family lawyers sent him any and all books he wanted. It was not often I could hit on any modern author in the category which pleased him most whom he didn't already know, but I discovered one day in conversation he had never heard of Arthur Machen. He sent for several of Machen's books, and a day or two later wrote a note to thank me. It was not unusual for him to write notes to people whom he saw four or five times a day. His typewriter was his principal toy. He usually delivered the notes himself, then walked away. I think it may be interesting to reproduce this particular note to fill in the picture of Phillip. We can call it *Self Portrait of a Dementia Praecox Case on First Reading the Works of Machen*, for this is what he wrote:

"Sweet spirits of my own dementia praecox! womb-wailing guidecalls reechoing throughout subcavernous-terraneans! fuga. fugae. cornucopious fugalations in depths in in in, in depths arbeitung verstaltheight. . . . I have just read the Hill of Dreams! By the brazen

buttocks of that brimstone bellona who lolls in lakes
of lava, never in my life have I read or even imagined
that such a piece of escapist literature existed. He is
superior to Dunsany and to Algernon Blackwood who
though almost not an escapist may be classed with
them. The book is filled with black magic. The man's
powers of psychotic invention are almost unbelievable
and his familiarity with certain phenomena of abnormal psychology is creepy. Are you acquainted with
Tchaikowski's scherzi? especially the waltz-scherzo of
his Fifth? It moves in this same, weird, uncanny way.
Now I wish I were dead."

XV

IT WAS during the flowering of my friendship with Phillip that I came to, and ultimately out of, the worst final crisis of my own. I had never quite wished, as he did of himself so frequently, that I were dead, but I began wishing again, violently, that I had never allowed myself to be locked up in a place of this sort. The new trouble centered round another fight with Dr. Quigley, but this time it concerned something more serious than prunes.

I had come into the place leaving a neglected, unfinished job in my own trade, and decided now one day that I had better stop enjoying myself in the carpentry shop and get going again on the piece of work which I had not only contracted to do, but had been partially paid for.

Paschall recommended that I be given the facilities and permission; it hung fire for a couple of mornings during which I worked in the carpenter shop as usual, and then the recommendation came back, vetoed by

Dr. Quigley. Since my trade was writing, and since all the equipment I needed was a typewriter and a few reams of paper, the veto surprised me, in fact surprised everybody. The reason it surprised everybody was that everybody was allowed to write all he wanted, and that typewriters, far from being taboo, were permitted to all patients, including the wildest ones on the worst back halls. Even patients who couldn't be trusted alone with pen or pencil were allowed use of bought or rented machines if they wanted them. Indeed the sound of pecking or tapping reassures the attendants that you're not up to mischief. Typewriters were favorite condoned toys in the asylum. Phillip had one, as related; Pontius Pilate had a portable; and Desogus's Chicken had an old Underwood on which he wrote long passionate love-poems signed Annabelle. I haven't yet introduced this elderly hermaphroditic gentleman whom we called "Desogus" for short. He was known as Desogus's Chicken because Spike had a psychiatric volume, by Leonardo Bianchi, in which a passage was quoted from Desogus which Spike felt described our friend quite aptly:

"It had the appearance of a hen, except that the neck was covered with masculine plumage; there was a comb and right wattle, and its deportment was that of a rooster. It copulated with the hens but was never heard to crow and never fought with other roosters. It laid eggs."

Take-a-letter Wylie had a heavy-duty Remington. He wrote letters continually, sometimes forty or fifty a day. He was his own stenographer and always said, "Take a letter," before he started tapping. He always had pockets filled with them when he came out in the park, and distributed them to any and everybody like handbills or Christmas cards, instructing us to mail them. We turned out floods of letters. Likewise a vast amount of "literature." At least three patients I knew were writing novels longer than *Anthony Adverse*, and the Reverend Mr. Higham specialized in short stories of the O. Henry school which he frequently read to us. He had invented a denouement technique which went the late O. Henry "one better" in a manner of speaking. Whereas the firecrackers which O. Henry habitually tied to the tails of his stories were generally only psychologically pyrotechnic, Mr. Higham always concluded his with real explosions. The automobile, the furnace in the cellar, or the kitchen stove always blew up with an actual bang and always brought the story to an end by the simple device of killing all the characters. He wrote two or three of them every week. They let him write all he wanted.

Dr. Quigley's refusal to let me write was therefore

so seemingly arbitrary that he took the trouble to come and see me about it, to tell me why he had refused. He had refused—of course for my own good, he said—for the precise reason that my trade was writing. I was welcome to a typewriter to play with, or write letters, but not to work on. All these others wrote, he said, as I, not being a carpenter, made chairs and tables; as our Wall Street contingent wove baskets, as wounded soldiers crocheted or did embroidery. It was bad occupational therapy, he said, for patients who were locked up under treatment, with hope of being cured, to work at the professions or trades they had followed outside. In other words, I mustn't write, because I was a writer!

"But don't you psychoanalytic cranks yourselves believe and teach that all writing, all art for that matter, is an escape-mechanism?"

"Yes," he said, "but that's beside the point. And you're not ready to escape yet. It will really be better for you to go on making chairs as an escape-diversion, and devote the serious part of yourself to facing your own problem instead of running away from it."

Of course, I got mad, lost my temper, and began to be unhappy again. I realized that by general rule, by blanket rule, by rule-of-thumb, his ruling was de-

fensible. But I hated general rules. I saw myself, as
every individual does, as an exception. I saw myself
caught in Quigley's damned red-taped cogs again. And,
of course, on top of it, disliking him, I naturally be-
lived, and still do, that he took a smug, sadistic pleasure in refusing to let me do what I wanted.

I went back to making chairs, but was worried and
unhappy. Paschall, my own doctor, told me candidly
that he didn't know . . . that it was quite possible
Quigley was right . . . that it might upset and harm
me to "go back to work" before I was cured.

This made me worry all the more. It is needless to
say that, for all my resentment, I didn't know either.
But it occurred to me that I must face it and try to
find out. It occurred to me that perhaps I had now
reached a point where it might be true that I must
either decide and do something for myself or disin-
tegrate. I had needed nurses, guardians, discipline
more desperately than any weak and wayward child,
but perhaps it was time to stop wrapping myself in
nursery symbolism, admit to myself that I was no authentic child but a hulking grown man gone wrong,
and that if I was to come out of this with anything
better than a carcass saved from cirrhosis of the liver,
I might have to do something about it myself. I didn't

want to do the wrong thing. It occurred to me that a good temporary thing to do might be to worry a while. So I set about deliberately worrying, just as one might set about picking apples or doing anagrams.

After a week of it, I asked for an interview with Quigley. He heard me patiently, if without sympathy. I explained to him that I had dug as deep into myself as I could and that I was afraid my trade had been the cause of my drunkenness. I was afraid, I told him, that what had driven me to drink was the fear that I could never write well enough for it to make any difference whether I wrote at all or not. If I went out in a few months apparently cured, started trying to write again, suffered from the old fear of futility and took to drink again, it would probably be the end of me, and nothing, incidentally, for him and his allegedly wonderful institution to be proud of. I felt it would be better and safer to try it here while I was locked up, under medical and psychiatric supervision, and couldn't drown my misery in gin no matter how unhappy my work made me.

Quigley heard me patiently, said he'd give the matter thought. In a couple of days his answer came back, "No." I was bitter about it and belly-ached about it to Spike and Charlie, to Phillip, to all my friends

among the patients and the staff. A fair majority of
the staff disliked Dr. Quigley as much as we did. We
buzzed. Notes were compared of many instances, some
trivial, some serious, in which it was agreed Quigley
had refused this and that request or plea for the pure
pleasure of refusing. We were surely unfair, unjust,
malicious toward him. But, allowing for all our own
dislike and prejudice, perhaps indeed because of them
—"giving the dog a bad name"—a picture of Quigley
emerged in which, though caricatured, there were lines
which showed, like his thin lips and sharp sniffing
nose, a tendency on his part to reach decisions thus:

"Dykeman has set his heart on doing so and so;
therefore, I'll forbid it."

Paschall still insisted that Quigley might be absolutely right in my case, but I knew he was not entirely
satisfied. Soon one day he said:

"Look here, would you feel any better about it if
it went before the staff? You might feel better if
Storm passed on it."

Storm was the big chief. We put it up to him. He
didn't know either, but he was big enough to telephone
my friend and publisher, Alfred Harcourt, admitting
he didn't know, and he was big enough then to say,
"Let's give the man a chance. Let's try it and see."

They gave me every chance. They were fine about it. I was still on Hall Two with Papa Duval who lent me an empty room, moved out the bed, found me a typewriter, table, fussed over me with proud misgivings like a clucking hen, and kept the carpet sweepers away from my door while I was tapping. They released me from work in the carpenter shop and gave me every "break" they could.

Inside of a week, I quite wished, like Phillip, that I were dead. It was the same old thing. I did my best, and it wasn't good enough. I don't mean that it wasn't good enough to print and perhaps interest some people and incidentally make some money. I mean specifically that it wasn't what I meant to write. Even when it came alive at times and flowed, it wasn't what I had meant. When it came alive a little, I felt a thrill and was happy, but always this was followed by a sense of frustration because, though the page or paragraph was alive and kicking, it wasn't the baby I had intended it to be. It was a different brat with a physiognomy other than I had wished it to have and toward whom I could feel neither warmth, pride nor affection. This was more painful than when the stuff was merely wooden, dead or awkward. When it was wooden, I knew it and could do something about it. But when it came alive, was the best I could do, and still was other than what I had meant it to be, I suffered a sort of agony that was futile, forlorn, yet resentful and desperate.

So there it was. It was this, or some form of it, that had made the neurasthenic pattern of my life, had made me finally a drunkard.

If I had been free now outside, I would surely have begun drinking again. Locked up where I couldn't get whiskey, I was forced to see sober a panorama that had been nothing but a miserable series of "runnings away from myself" since earliest childhood, and in which, I now fully realized for the first time, neither whiskey nor the particular trade I had adopted were anything more than incidental. I took sober stock and saw that dissatisfaction, a sense of my own inability to arrive at a harmonious adjustment in any environment—sporadically dotted with flights and attempted escapes—had been the whole pattern of my life. I had run away ineffectually at six to be a pirate as all children do, and instead of getting maturer powers of adjustment as I grew older, I had been running away ever since. At twenty I had run away to be a tramp. Later, with no better motive, I had run away to war. I had run away to the East and West

Indies, to the Arabian desert, the Kurdistan mountains, the jungles of Africa. I had run as far as Timbuctoo, and had stumped my toe, and had hurt it so badly that I ran away once more with a bottle, to be a drunkard and forget it. I had said on all these occasions, sometimes proudly, that I had been running *to* some place or some thing, had invented plausible reasons and produced by-products. Now I knew that all the time I had been running away *from* something, and that the thing had always been myself. And now I was locked up where I couldn't run away, either by boat or bottle. I had to stay with myself and look at myself and it wasn't pleasant. I saw, for one thing, that I had nothing to blame on whiskey, nor even on intoxication, which may sometimes be divine. Whiskey was a gift of the gods—dangerous, like fire and all gifts from heaven—to be used by the strong man with pleasure for joy, to solace and stimulate the imagination, to clothe reality in rosy light, evoke elusive happiness. I had misused it as a stupefying poison, to deaden consciousness—as an escape.

And even this escape, in common with all my attempts, had been futile. I hadn't liked being a drunkard any more than I had liked the town where I was born—or Timbuctoo. I didn't like it drunk or sober. I just didn't like it.

In that case, never having cared for suicide, and doubting that I would like being dead any better than being alive, if as well, the only stupid, decent thing to do about it seemed to be to make the best of it. For instance, one thing might be to try to stop moaning subconsciously that I hadn't been born an artist and get on with the job I had to do as a more or less competent artisan. That seemed to be indicated.

So I went back to work on that new basis, right there in the asylum. I had to tear up a lot of it, as usual, because it was wooden, and when parts of it came alive, as usual, they were not alive in the way I had meant them to be and it was then that I frequently almost wished, like Phillip, that I were dead. I finally finished it as best I could, and it has since been published. Long months have now elapsed since then. At the time I am writing this chapter, I have been out of the asylum, discharged as cured, for more than six months, and I seem to be actually cured of alcoholism, but the rest of it hasn't changed at all. It is all just the same as it used to be—except that I have a better idea now what it's about. I don't like it any better than I used to.

I liked it so little during the first ensuing weeks in the asylum—after I had gone to work—that I began to wonder whether it was any use to keep on writing—

whether a solution might be to get another trade or go into business. But I began to notice one thing, apart from the writing and the worry connected with not being able to write as I wanted. (On that score, it was no use to tell myself that I took myself too damned seriously, for it was writing I took seriously rather than myself. If I never had been and never will be anything but a reporter, I still take writing seriously. I am not ashamed of that. I can't do anything about it and I wouldn't want to if I could.) What I began to notice, apart from such matters, was that life was more pleasant, more tolerable, sober than it had ever been while I was drinking. It was now summer, and I was taking pleasure in many things I had ceased to care for. I was playing tennis again, better than I had for years, and was enjoying golf again though I knew I'd always be a dub at it. Furthermore I was enjoying waking up in the morning, and enjoying breakfast which I had loathed ever since I could remember. I enjoyed despising Dr. Quigley and liking Dr. Paschall. I began answering letters and began thinking I might enjoy seeing my friends in the outside world again. But most of all, I enjoyed my now familiar present friends, my fellow-inmates, so much that I sometimes wondered whether I'd find my sane friends as congenial.

In June, seeing me more cheerful, better coördinated, they moved me from Hall Two into one of the convalescent "villas," and from that time on I was practically as free, within the confines of the park, as I would have been in a summer hotel or colony. I liked it so well, including the being sober, the going to bed never befuddled and never awakening in the morning with a hangover, that I felt as a matter of pleasure-preference that when I got out I'd probably live generally sober, no matter how worried or depressed I ever became over work which wouldn't come right. To that personal problem, still taking writing seriously in the abstract, I could say, "Who gives a damn?" and answer, "Nobody." There were plenty of good writers. Too many, maybe. I could go on trying to do my best, and if I never got to be one of the good ones, it would be a purely private misfortune. I'd doubtless find something new to worry about, something new to run away from . . . but I had dragged this out and taken it to pieces and looked at it, and, though it made me sad, I didn't think I'd be afraid of it any more.

But would I be afraid of whiskey when I got out? Ought I to be afraid of it? Ought I to let it alone entirely? I didn't know, and I soon discovered that the doctors didn't know either. I discovered not only that the doctors in this institution didn't know, but that nobody seemed to know. A few of the world's leading doctors and psychiatrists are didactic and claim to know, but the trouble is that their opinions are widely divergent. One tiny, gloomy group stick to the old Latin dictum, "Once a drunkard always a drunkard," and aver that no drunkard has ever been permanently cured or ever will be. If they were right, it would make no eventual difference whether I went out afraid of whiskey and tried to let it alone or not. It would get me sooner or later anyway. Another group, the "Boston group," takes its stand on a new arbitrary dictum from which it contends there is no appeal:

"Once a drunkard always a drunkard—or a teetotaler."

Still another group, equally didactic and distinguished—and decidedly less pessimistic—believes that both these dictums are pure nonsense, that it is possible, though difficult, to cure a drunkard, and that if he is cured, being cured, he can drink again without danger.

Thus, on the subject of "Drunkards," scientific opinion is contradictory and divergent. On the subject of drinking, which is an entirely different, though related, subject, there is more agreement. There is general agreement, for instance, among all authorities on the following points:

"That alcohol is a narcotic, which, by depressing
the higher centers, removes inhibitions, thereby producing a sense of freedom, a feeling of well-being,
but obviously also rendering the drinker less 'responsible' and therefore constituting a danger.

"That while it may stimulate imagination, it never
increases intelligence or skill, but on the contrary im-
pairs reason, will, self-control, judgment, physical
skill and endurance.

"That it does not increase and sometimes decreases
the body's resistance to infection; that it's therapeutic
usefulness and value are slight.

"That it is improbable that it has injured, in the
long run, the quality of human stock, but that its individual effects are often devastating.

"That, in addition to being a narcotic, it is a definite
poison when absorbed in sufficient quantities which
vary with the individual, producing successively ex-
citation, incoördination, stupor, coma, death."

Why, being agreed that it's a poison, do so large
and distinguished a proportion of the medical-scien-
tific fraternity as well as the world in general, continue
to enjoy their cocktails? Or why, in fact, do you? On
this paradoxical point, the medical psychologists are in
broad-minded agreement. They point out that a sense

of well-being is a sense of well-being even though
toxically induced, and are even fair enough to admit,
of the fellow who absorbs and enjoys eleven cocktails
instead of one and pays for it with a nervous breakdown or worse, that "ecstasy is ecstasy even when
toxic."

Dr. Adolf Meyer of Johns Hopkins says cautiously
of moderate, decent drinking:

"It is a relief from tension, though not a construc-
tive help."

They doubt, but are not agreed, that drinking has
ever made a drunkard. Hyman and his followers are
sure that chronic alcoholism, whether among intellectuals or illiterate bums on the Bowery, is "always a
symptom of some other underlying psychic disorder."

Because of all this, it seemed to me, and I said so,
that to go out and never be able to touch a cocktail,
glass of wine or highball again would be a poor sort
of cure, if it could indeed be termed a cure at all. I
said that I still hoped to be really "cured," cured so
well that I would be able not only to take a highball
with my friends, but even on appropriate occasions to
take several and cut up high jinks. They were extremely dubious. They invited me cordially to remain
another six months under renewed voluntary commitment, in the villa, and said that at the end of that

time they might have an opinion. I cordially accepted. I liked it there, and was enjoying not drinking. I seemed to be being cured. It was my friends on the outside who became dubious in their turn about my remaining in an institution for so long a period. Conferences were held, and the loyal hard-boiled friend who had first had the bright idea of locking me up in an asylum, developed another bright idea that met everybody's approval, including mine, and including . . . which was more important . . . the approval of the entire institution staff, with the exception of Dr. Quigley. They were to give me a clean discharge, turn me loose as cured, but I was to agree of my own volition, as an experiment, to promise to go six full additional months without touching a drop of alcohol in any form. Did that mean wine and beer? Yes, it meant everything. I was quite willing, just as I'd been equally willing to stay there another half year. They exacted no parole promise that if I failed in my main promise I'd come back to them. But they promised on their part that if I fell in the ditch they'd let me come back. My hard-boiled friend said I wouldn't be worth taking back but that if I fell in the United States I'd be thrown back—just once, as a favor, for friendship's sake, then hands washed of it forever.

So one day late in June we waved good-by. I went

to the country. I continued to play tennis and golf, continued to work at my writing and continued to worry that I couldn't write better. Friends drank at the golf club, friends drank at the house where I lived and in the town where we frequently went to the movies. In August I went fishing down in Maine, returned and started writing and worrying again. The Armenian was still an Armenian. There was nothing anybody could do about that. I haven't a very good memory for dates, and the six months elapsed without my noting it. Except for wishing that I might drink beer on a few exceptionally hot occasions in midsummer, I hadn't thought much about it one way or another. I had some new things to worry about, and I had gotten out of the habit of drinking. A fortnight or so after the six months had elapsed somebody brought out a bottle of Spanish sherry. It occurred to me that it would be a good thing to try first, after so long an abstinence. I had a glass and liked it very much. It brought a pleasant glow. We were soon at dinner. It didn't occur to me to want more of it. I can say this now, but when interested questions were asked at the time, I found it difficult to answer them. The truest answer I could get at was that it hadn't occurred to me even not to want more of it. Some days later, being thirsty, I was pleased to be drinking a glass of beer instead of Coca-Cola. One night driving in the cold, we came home and had a shot of whiskey. I liked that too. And on another night, playing chess until late, we had highballs. They were pleasant enough, but I don't think I cared much. Apparently, when I was a drunkard, I had been guzzling whiskey in a different way for a different reason. Months have passed now since I first took those rare drinks, and I still drink rarely. I don't think I worry much about it. I have other worries. But I am less unhappy than I used to be when I tried to drown them. I seem to be cured of drunkenness, which is as may be.

ABOUT THE ARTIST

From Doug Wright Award winner Joe Ollmann, author of the bestselling graphic novel, *Mid-Life,* published by Drawn and Quarterly, comes a new Introduction and cover art in celebration of this 2015 Dover edition of *Asylum* by William Seabrook.

A CATALOG OF SELECTED DOVER BOOKS IN ALL FIELDS OF INTEREST

100 BEST-LOVED POEMS, Edited by Philip Smith. "The Passionate Shepherd to His Love," "Shall I compare thee to a summer's day?" "Death, be not proud," "The Raven," "The Road Not Taken," plus works by Blake, Wordsworth, Byron, Shelley, Keats, many others. 96pp. 5³⁄₁₆ x 8¼. 0-486-28553-7

100 SMALL HOUSES OF THE THIRTIES, Brown-Blodgett Company. Exterior photographs and floor plans for 100 charming structures. Illustrations of models accompanied by descriptions of interiors, color schemes, closet space, and other amenities. 200 illustrations. 112pp. 8⅜ x 11. 0-486-44131-8

1000 TURN-OF-THE-CENTURY HOUSES: With Illustrations and Floor Plans, Herbert C. Chivers. Reproduced from a rare edition, this showcase of homes ranges from cottages and bungalows to sprawling mansions. Each house is meticulously illustrated and accompanied by complete floor plans. 256pp. 9⅜ x 12¼. 0-486-45596-3

101 GREAT AMERICAN POEMS, Edited by The American Poetry & Literacy Project. Rich treasury of verse from the 19th and 20th centuries includes works by Edgar Allan Poe, Robert Frost, Walt Whitman, Langston Hughes, Emily Dickinson, T. S. Eliot, other notables. 96pp. 5³⁄₁₆ x 8¼. 0-486-40158-8

101 GREAT SAMURAI PRINTS, Utagawa Kuniyoshi. Kuniyoshi was a master of the warrior woodblock print — and these 18th-century illustrations represent the pinnacle of his craft. Full-color portraits of renowned Japanese samurais pulse with movement, passion, and remarkably fine detail. 112pp. 8⅜ x 11. 0-486-46523-3

ABC OF BALLET, Janet Grosser. Clearly worded, abundantly illustrated little guide defines basic ballet-related terms: arabesque, battement, pas de chat, relevé, sissonne, many others. Pronunciation guide included. Excellent primer. 48pp. 4⁵⁄₁₆ x 5¾. 0-486-40871-X

ACCESSORIES OF DRESS: An Illustrated Encyclopedia, Katherine Lester and Bess Viola Oerke. Illustrations of hats, veils, wigs, cravats, shawls, shoes, gloves, and other accessories enhance an engaging commentary that reveals the humor and charm of the many-sided story of accessorized apparel. 644 figures and 59 plates. 608pp. 6 ⅛ x 9¼. 0-486-43378-1

ADVENTURES OF HUCKLEBERRY FINN, Mark Twain. Join Huck and Jim as their boyhood adventures along the Mississippi River lead them into a world of excitement, danger, and self-discovery. Humorous narrative, lyrical descriptions of the Mississippi valley, and memorable characters. 224pp. 5³⁄₁₆ x 8¼. 0-486-28061-6

ALICE STARMORE'S BOOK OF FAIR ISLE KNITTING, Alice Starmore. A noted designer from the region of Scotland's Fair Isle explores the history and techniques of this distinctive, stranded-color knitting style and provides copious illustrated instructions for 14 original knitwear designs. 208pp. 8⅜ x 10⅞. 0-486-47218-3

Browse over 9,000 books at www.doverpublications.com

ALICE'S ADVENTURES IN WONDERLAND, Lewis Carroll. Beloved classic about a little girl lost in a topsy-turvy land and her encounters with the White Rabbit, March Hare, Mad Hatter, Cheshire Cat, and other delightfully improbable characters. 42 illustrations by Sir John Tenniel. 96pp. 5³⁄₁₆ x 8¼. 0-486-27543-4

AMERICA'S LIGHTHOUSES: An Illustrated History, Francis Ross Holland. Profusely illustrated fact-filled survey of American lighthouses since 1716. Over 200 stations — East, Gulf, and West coasts, Great Lakes, Hawaii, Alaska, Puerto Rico, the Virgin Islands, and the Mississippi and St. Lawrence Rivers. 240pp. 8 x 10¾.
0-486-25576-X

AN ENCYCLOPEDIA OF THE VIOLIN, Alberto Bachmann. Translated by Frederick H. Martens. Introduction by Eugene Ysaye. First published in 1925, this renowned reference remains unsurpassed as a source of essential information, from construction and evolution to repertoire and technique. Includes a glossary and 73 illustrations. 496pp. 6½ x 9¼. 0-486-46618-3

ANIMALS: 1,419 Copyright-Free Illustrations of Mammals, Birds, Fish, Insects, etc., Selected by Jim Harter. Selected for its visual impact and ease of use, this outstanding collection of wood engravings presents over 1,000 species of animals in extremely lifelike poses. Includes mammals, birds, reptiles, amphibians, fish, insects, and other invertebrates. 284pp. 9 x 12. 0-486-23766-4

THE ANNALS, Tacitus. Translated by Alfred John Church and William Jackson Brodribb. This vital chronicle of Imperial Rome, written by the era's great historian, spans A.D. 14-68 and paints incisive psychological portraits of major figures, from Tiberius to Nero. 416pp. 5³⁄₁₆ x 8¼. 0-486-45236-0

ANTIGONE, Sophocles. Filled with passionate speeches and sensitive probing of moral and philosophical issues, this powerful and often-performed Greek drama reveals the grim fate that befalls the children of Oedipus. Footnotes. 64pp. 5³⁄₁₆ x 8 ¼. 0-486-27804-2

ART DECO DECORATIVE PATTERNS IN FULL COLOR, Christian Stoll. Reprinted from a rare 1910 portfolio, 160 sensuous and exotic images depict a breathtaking array of florals, geometrics, and abstracts — all elegant in their stark simplicity. 64pp. 8⅜ x 11. 0-486-44862-2

THE ARTHUR RACKHAM TREASURY: 86 Full-Color Illustrations, Arthur Rackham. Selected and Edited by Jeff A. Menges. A stunning treasury of 86 full-page plates span the famed English artist's career, from *Rip Van Winkle* (1905) to masterworks such as *Undine, A Midsummer Night's Dream,* and *Wind in the Willows* (1939). 96pp. 8⅜ x 11.
0-486-44685-9

THE AUTHENTIC GILBERT & SULLIVAN SONGBOOK, W. S. Gilbert and A. S. Sullivan. The most comprehensive collection available, this songbook includes selections from every one of Gilbert and Sullivan's light operas. Ninety-two numbers are presented uncut and unedited, and in their original keys. 410pp. 9 x 12.
0-486-23482-7

THE AWAKENING, Kate Chopin. First published in 1899, this controversial novel of a New Orleans wife's search for love outside a stifling marriage shocked readers. Today, it remains a first-rate narrative with superb characterization. New introductory Note. 128pp. 5³⁄₁₆ x 8¼. 0-486-27786-0

BASIC DRAWING, Louis Priscilla. Beginning with perspective, this commonsense manual progresses to the figure in movement, light and shade, anatomy, drapery, composition, trees and landscape, and outdoor sketching. Black-and-white illustrations throughout. 128pp. 8⅜ x 11. 0-486-45815-6

Browse over 9,000 books at www.doverpublications.com

THE BATTLES THAT CHANGED HISTORY, Fletcher Pratt. Historian profiles 16 crucial conflicts, ancient to modern, that changed the course of Western civilization. Gripping accounts of battles led by Alexander the Great, Joan of Arc, Ulysses S. Grant, other commanders. 27 maps. 352pp. 5⅜ x 8½.   0-486-41129-X

BEETHOVEN'S LETTERS, Ludwig van Beethoven. Edited by Dr. A. C. Kalischer. Features 457 letters to fellow musicians, friends, greats, patrons, and literary men. Reveals musical thoughts, quirks of personality, insights, and daily events. Includes 15 plates. 410pp. 5⅜ x 8½.   0-486-22769-3

BERNICE BOBS HER HAIR AND OTHER STORIES, F. Scott Fitzgerald. This brilliant anthology includes 6 of Fitzgerald's most popular stories: "The Diamond as Big as the Ritz," the title tale, "The Offshore Pirate," "The Ice Palace," "The Jelly Bean," and "May Day." 176pp. 5⅜ x 8½.   0-486-47049-0

BESLER'S BOOK OF FLOWERS AND PLANTS: 73 Full-Color Plates from Hortus Eystettensis, 1613, Basilius Besler. Here is a selection of magnificent plates from the *Hortus Eystettensis*, which vividly illustrated and identified the plants, flowers, and trees that thrived in the legendary German garden at Eichstätt. 80pp. 8⅜ x 11.
0-486-46005-3

THE BOOK OF KELLS, Edited by Blanche Cirker. Painstakingly reproduced from a rare facsimile edition, this volume contains full-page decorations, portraits, illustrations, plus a sampling of textual leaves with exquisite calligraphy and ornamentation. 32 full-color illustrations. 32pp. 9⅜ x 12¼.   0-486-24345-1

THE BOOK OF THE CROSSBOW: With an Additional Section on Catapults and Other Siege Engines, Ralph Payne-Gallwey. Fascinating study traces history and use of crossbow as military and sporting weapon, from Middle Ages to modern times. Also covers related weapons: balistas, catapults, Turkish bows, more. Over 240 illustrations. 400pp. 7¼ x 10⅛.   0-486-28720-3

THE BUNGALOW BOOK: Floor Plans and Photos of 112 Houses, 1910, Henry L. Wilson. Here are 112 of the most popular and economic blueprints of the early 20th century — plus an illustration or photograph of each completed house. A wonderful time capsule that still offers a wealth of valuable insights. 160pp. 8⅜ x 11.
0-486-45104-6

THE CALL OF THE WILD, Jack London. A classic novel of adventure, drawn from London's own experiences as a Klondike adventurer, relating the story of a heroic dog caught in the brutal life of the Alaska Gold Rush. Note. 64pp. 5³⁄₁₆ x 8¼.
0-486-26472-6

CANDIDE, Voltaire. Edited by Francois-Marie Arouet. One of the world's great satires since its first publication in 1759. Witty, caustic skewering of romance, science, philosophy, religion, government — nearly all human ideals and institutions. 112pp. 5³⁄₁₆ x 8¼.   0-486-26689-3

CELEBRATED IN THEIR TIME: Photographic Portraits from the George Grantham Bain Collection, Edited by Amy Pastan. With an Introduction by Michael Carlebach. Remarkable portrait gallery features 112 rare images of Albert Einstein, Charlie Chaplin, the Wright Brothers, Henry Ford, and other luminaries from the worlds of politics, art, entertainment, and industry. 128pp. 8⅜ x 11.   0-486-46754-6

CHARIOTS FOR APOLLO: The NASA History of Manned Lunar Spacecraft to 1969, Courtney G. Brooks, James M. Grimwood, and Loyd S. Swenson, Jr. This illustrated history by a trio of experts is the definitive reference on the Apollo spacecraft and lunar modules. It traces the vehicles' design, development, and operation in space. More than 100 photographs and illustrations. 576pp. 6¾ x 9¼. 0-486-46756-2

Browse over 9,000 books at www.doverpublications.com

A CHRISTMAS CAROL, Charles Dickens. This engrossing tale relates Ebenezer Scrooge's ghostly journeys through Christmases past, present, and future and his ultimate transformation from a harsh and grasping old miser to a charitable and compassionate human being. 80pp. 5³⁄₁₆ x 8¼. 0-486-26865-9

COMMON SENSE, Thomas Paine. First published in January of 1776, this highly influential landmark document clearly and persuasively argued for American separation from Great Britain and paved the way for the Declaration of Independence. 64pp. 5³⁄₁₆ x 8¼. 0-486-29602-4

THE COMPLETE SHORT STORIES OF OSCAR WILDE, Oscar Wilde. Complete texts of "The Happy Prince and Other Tales," "A House of Pomegranates," "Lord Arthur Savile's Crime and Other Stories," "Poems in Prose," and "The Portrait of Mr. W. H." 208pp. 5³⁄₁₆ x 8¼. 0-486-45216-6

COMPLETE SONNETS, William Shakespeare. Over 150 exquisite poems deal with love, friendship, the tyranny of time, beauty's evanescence, death, and other themes in language of remarkable power, precision, and beauty. Glossary of archaic terms. 80pp. 5³⁄₁₆ x 8¼. 0-486-26686-9

THE COUNT OF MONTE CRISTO: Abridged Edition, Alexandre Dumas. Falsely accused of treason, Edmond Dantès is imprisoned in the bleak Chateau d'If. After a hair-raising escape, he launches an elaborate plot to extract a bitter revenge against those who betrayed him. 448pp. 5³⁄₁₆ x 8¼. 0-486-45643-9

CRAFTSMAN BUNGALOWS: Designs from the Pacific Northwest, Yoho & Merritt. This reprint of a rare catalog, showcasing the charming simplicity and cozy style of Craftsman bungalows, is filled with photos of completed homes, plus floor plans and estimated costs. An indispensable resource for architects, historians, and illustrators. 112pp. 10 x 7. 0-486-46875-5

CRAFTSMAN BUNGALOWS: 59 Homes from "The Craftsman," Edited by Gustav Stickley. Best and most attractive designs from Arts and Crafts Movement publication — 1903–1916 — includes sketches, photographs of homes, floor plans, descriptive text. 128pp. 8¼ x 11. 0-486-25829-7

CRIME AND PUNISHMENT, Fyodor Dostoyevsky. Translated by Constance Garnett. Supreme masterpiece tells the story of Raskolnikov, a student tormented by his own thoughts after he murders an old woman. Overwhelmed by guilt and terror, he confesses and goes to prison. 480pp. 5³⁄₁₆ x 8¼. 0-486-41587-2

THE DECLARATION OF INDEPENDENCE AND OTHER GREAT DOCUMENTS OF AMERICAN HISTORY: 1775-1865, Edited by John Grafton. Thirteen compelling and influential documents: Henry's "Give Me Liberty or Give Me Death," Declaration of Independence, The Constitution, Washington's First Inaugural Address, The Monroe Doctrine, The Emancipation Proclamation, Gettysburg Address, more. 64pp. 5³⁄₁₆ x 8¼. 0-486-41124-9

THE DESERT AND THE SOWN: Travels in Palestine and Syria, Gertrude Bell. "The female Lawrence of Arabia," Gertrude Bell wrote captivating, perceptive accounts of her travels in the Middle East. This intriguing narrative, accompanied by 160 photos, traces her 1905 sojourn in Lebanon, Syria, and Palestine. 368pp. 5⅜ x 8½. 0-486-46876-3

A DOLL'S HOUSE, Henrik Ibsen. Ibsen's best-known play displays his genius for realistic prose drama. An expression of women's rights, the play climaxes when the central character, Nora, rejects a smothering marriage and life in "a doll's house." 80pp. 5³⁄₁₆ x 8¼. 0-486-27062-9

DOOMED SHIPS: Great Ocean Liner Disasters, William H. Miller, Jr. Nearly 200 photographs, many from private collections, highlight tales of some of the vessels whose pleasure cruises ended in catastrophe: the *Morro Castle, Normandie, Andrea Doria, Europa,* and many others. 128pp. 8⅞ x 11¾.　　0-486-45366-9

THE DORÉ BIBLE ILLUSTRATIONS, Gustave Doré. Detailed plates from the Bible: the Creation scenes, Adam and Eve, horrifying visions of the Flood, the battle sequences with their monumental crowds, depictions of the life of Jesus, 241 plates in all. 241pp. 9 x 12.　　0-486-23004-X

DRAWING DRAPERY FROM HEAD TO TOE, Cliff Young. Expert guidance on how to draw shirts, pants, skirts, gloves, hats, and coats on the human figure, including folds in relation to the body, pull and crush, action folds, creases, more. Over 200 drawings. 48pp. 8¼ x 11.　　0-486-45591-2

DUBLINERS, James Joyce. A fine and accessible introduction to the work of one of the 20th century's most influential writers, this collection features 15 tales, including a masterpiece of the short-story genre, "The Dead." 160pp. 5³⁄₁₆ x 8¼.

0-486-26870-5

EASY-TO-MAKE POP-UPS, Joan Irvine. Illustrated by Barbara Reid. Dozens of wonderful ideas for three-dimensional paper fun — from holiday greeting cards with moving parts to a pop-up menagerie. Easy-to-follow, illustrated instructions for more than 30 projects. 299 black-and-white illustrations. 96pp. 8⅜ x 11.

0-486-44622-0

EASY-TO-MAKE STORYBOOK DOLLS: A "Novel" Approach to Cloth Dollmaking, Sherralyn St. Clair. Favorite fictional characters come alive in this unique beginner's dollmaking guide. Includes patterns for Pollyanna, Dorothy from *The Wonderful Wizard of Oz,* Mary of *The Secret Garden,* plus easy-to-follow instructions, 263 black-and-white illustrations, and an 8-page color insert. 112pp. 8¼ x 11.　0-486-47360-0

EINSTEIN'S ESSAYS IN SCIENCE, Albert Einstein. Speeches and essays in accessible, everyday language profile influential physicists such as Niels Bohr and Isaac Newton. They also explore areas of physics to which the author made major contributions. 128pp. 5 x 8.　　0-486-47011-3

EL DORADO: Further Adventures of the Scarlet Pimpernel, Baroness Orczy. A popular sequel to *The Scarlet Pimpernel,* this suspenseful story recounts the Pimpernel's attempts to rescue the Dauphin from imprisonment during the French Revolution. An irresistible blend of intrigue, period detail, and vibrant characterizations. 352pp. 5³⁄₁₆ x 8¼.　　0-486-44026-5

ELEGANT SMALL HOMES OF THE TWENTIES: 99 Designs from a Competition, Chicago Tribune. Nearly 100 designs for five- and six-room houses feature New England and Southern colonials, Normandy cottages, stately Italianate dwellings, and other fascinating snapshots of American domestic architecture of the 1920s. 112pp. 9 x 12.　　0-486-46910-7

THE ELEMENTS OF STYLE: The Original Edition, William Strunk, Jr. This is the book that generations of writers have relied upon for timeless advice on grammar, diction, syntax, and other essentials. In concise terms, it identifies the principal requirements of proper style and common errors. 64pp. 5⅜ x 8½.　0-486-44798-7

THE ELUSIVE PIMPERNEL, Baroness Orczy. Robespierre's revolutionaries find their wicked schemes thwarted by the heroic Pimpernel — Sir Percival Blakeney. In this thrilling sequel, Chauvelin devises a plot to eliminate the Pimpernel and his wife. 272pp. 5³⁄₁₆ x 8¼.　　0-486-45464-9